There are some stories that inspire us, some that heal us, and others that transform us. Dean Otto's story is so powerful that it does all of those things. As a communications professional, I've shared countless stories that help others, but never one that had an impact like Dean's. I can say with confidence that working with Dean changed my life and gave me a perspective on the human spirit that I'm incredibly grateful for. Dean's perseverance and relentless ability to fight against all the odds will light a fire in everyone who opens their hearts to his story.

Claire Simmons

Director of Clinical Communications, Atrium Health

Defying all odds! *2% Chance* is a dynamic story of resilience that will leave you inspired to think beyond capabilities. Around every corner of Dean Otto's journey is proof that the road less traveled can lead to avenues of hope when least expected. When life decides to take a turn, embrace the bumpy ride, for there is good up ahead!

Jodie Morrow

Director of Strategy and Communications,
Stryker Orthopaedics and Spine Group

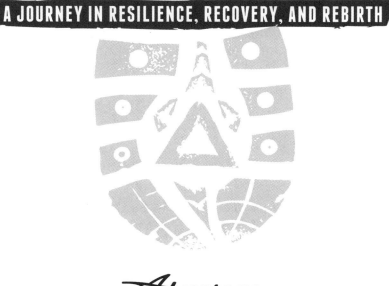

DEAN OTTO

2%

CHANCE

A JOURNEY IN RESILIENCE, RECOVERY, AND REBIRTH

Advantage®

Published by Advantage, Charleston, South Carolina.
Member of Advantage Media Group.

ADVANTAGE is a registered trademark, and the Advantage colophon is a trademark of Advantage Media Group, Inc.

Printed in the United States of America.

10 9 8 7 6 5 4 3 2 1

ISBN: 978-1-64225-272-9
LCCN: 2021914369

Cover design by Megan Elger.
Layout design by Wesley Strickland.

This publication is designed to provide accurate and authoritative information in regard to the subject matter covered. It is sold with the understanding that the publisher is not engaged in rendering legal, accounting, or other professional services. If legal advice or other expert assistance is required, the services of a competent professional person should be sought.

 Advantage Media Group is proud to be a part of the Tree Neutral® program. Tree Neutral offsets the number of trees consumed in the production and printing of this book by taking proactive steps such as planting trees in direct proportion to the number of trees used to print books. To learn more about Tree Neutral, please visit **www.treeneutral.com**.

Advantage Media Group is a publisher of business, self-improvement, and professional development books and online learning. We help entrepreneurs, business leaders, and professionals share their Stories, Passion, and Knowledge to help others Learn & Grow. Do you have a manuscript or book idea that you would like us to consider for publishing? Please visit **advantagefamily.com**.

It doesn't matter what is under your Christmas tree;
it matters who is around it. I dedicate this book to my
entire family—without you I am nothing.

CONTENTS

ACKNOWLEDGMENTS

The following folks' love and support made this book possible: God; my family—Beth, Will, and Grace Otto; Richard, Jan, and Stacy Otto; Kay Matton; Sue and Bill Long; Scott, Pam, and Skylar Hodges; David and Stacy and Josh Hodges; Jack, Diana Ella, and Liam Jordan; Christine, Jack, and Aiden Choate; and Mike and Gail Wales.

The two men and their wives who made this story what it is: Matt and Laura McGirt, and Will and Jeanelle Huffman—amazing people whom I hold in the highest regard.

Medical team: the amazing team of doctors, nurses, and therapists at Carolina Neurosurgery and Spine Associates, especially Dr. Matt McGirt and Graham Claytor. The trauma and rehab teams at Atrium Health Carolinas Rehabilitation: all these people did their jobs in the moment, and without them I had no chance for recovery. The marketing team at Atrium, especially Claire Hossman and Wendy Fu. And thanks to my therapists at Atrium Rehab: Jennelle St. Claire and Jackie LaBarbera.

Media team: Jodie Morrow at Stryker Spine, Michelle Boudin at WCNC Charlotte, and Théoden Janes at the *Charlotte Observer*. Tracy Gold and Jenny Revell at *The Ellen Show*, Hannah Van Winkle and Harry Smith at the *Today* show on NBC. All these folks are amazing people, storytellers, and professionals.

Thanks to Neil Lustig, Cassie Young, and the entire company at my former employer for their support as I made my comeback. They had my back and allowed me my space and time to recover.

Thanks to Dr. Scott Greenapple for putting Humpty Dumpty back together again for years before and after the accident. To my coach, Kelly Fillnow, for her amazing coaching and spiritual support. And Anne Hitchell for working the kinks out with her insanely awesome massage.

Thank you to the men on Saturday morning and Wednesday night, and all the folks at Myers Park. You are my spiritual beacons.

Thanks to Pat Forquer, my friend and current boss, for all his support and guidance at Braze and for putting up with me while writing this book!

Thank you to all my friends who have supported me, cheered for me, and loved me, in good times and bad. I'm the wealthiest man alive with friends, and to list you all would make another book! I'd like to specially call out Paul and Betsy Parker, Caroline and Larry Wilson, Nels Schlander, Mark Baldwin, Sandy Solomon, Chris Harpeneau, Jeff LaPiana, Kenny Mollica, David Schneider, John Kallis, Tim Parsons, Scott and Jill Ilario, Jim and Nina Pulliam, Fred and Amy Parker, Tony Ricardo, Zach Hughes, Josh Heiskell, and Drew Harkey. You all were there when it mattered most. And thank you to Brian Muscarella—you inspire me!

Thanks to Todd Caponi, Tricia Manning, and Steve Gilliland—you all believed in me.

Finally, the team at Advantage: Chip St. Clair for his amazing leadership and collaboration on this book, Laura Rashley and Laura Grinstead for all their help and guidance putting the book together, Megan Elger for her cover design, and Keith Kopcsak for getting me in the boat!

INTRODUCTION

I've never fancied myself a writer. Growing up, English was my least favorite subject. I didn't have much interest in writing. Or reading. I liked math. And sports. Writing, however, was a chore—something assigned in school. Never something I would do voluntarily.

After my accident and subsequent recovery, my family, especially my wife, Beth, and my sister, Stacy, encouraged me to write this book. Many friends and coworkers, not to mention folks in the media, said, "Dean, you have to write about your journey. This is a story that needs to be told. You can inspire so many people to overcome obstacles in their lives." That's all great, but like I said: I'm not a writer. And I don't have a lot of free time. And I didn't want to look like I was riding the gravy train.

But I wanted to help people.

The year after my accident went by really fast. After a severe spinal cord injury like mine, you have about eighteen months to basically get back all you are ever going to get back. So the race was on. Literally. I was super focused on getting back everything that I could as fast as I could. Which meant I had to work my tail off every day in rehab with Graham Claytor, then after that on my own with the help of my coach, Kelly Fillnow. No time to write a book.

Then, one morning about three years ago, my family and I were on vacation in Hopetown, Bahamas. My son, Will, was flying in, and I had to take the ferry over to Marsh Harbor to pick him up. It had been quite a journey for him. His flight was diverted to Nassau, so he had to stay the night there by himself while we were vacationing with our good friends, the Hundleys. He missed out on the first day, so I wanted to be there for him when he landed. Of course, the flight was late, and I had some time to kill. So I thought, *this would be a great time to start writing the book.* I was by myself for a few hours in a beautiful place. So I pulled out my phone and began typing with my thumbs.

I shared what I had written with Beth, Stacy, and a couple of friends. Théoden Janes—a writer for the *Charlotte Observer*, a fellow runner, and my friend—had written a story about me, the doctor who saved me, and the man who hit me. That article came out the morning of September 24, 2017—exactly one year after the accident that left me paralyzed. Théoden and the others liked what I had written, so I kept at it. A little at a time. A chapter every few weeks. Eventually, I stopped.

Then, sometime in early 2020, I finally had the epiphany I needed. By that time, I had given so many speeches about our story. Nothing gave me more joy than sharing it with others and inspiring them. Seeing people's reactions—their smiles, their tears, the connection we made. It was incredible. I felt like Mick Jagger on stage! So that's when I had the thought: *Do you want to do something truly meaningful in your life? Do you want to be able to change lives and help others?*

I stopped making excuses and just made it happen. So here we are.

I once heard a quote from the Dalai Lama when he was asked about the meaning of life. To paraphrase, he said, "We're all here to have fun and to help each other." Nothing gives me a better feeling than helping others. I hope you read this book and are inspired, helped, and most importantly, inspired to help others.

Happy reading!

CHAPTER ONE:
THE PAIN

Growing up, all I ever wanted to do was belong. I wanted to feel a part of the group and wanted people to like me. Whether that was being the cool kid in the neighborhood, the one with the house where everyone wanted to hang out, or the popular and funny kid in school, I wanted to be that guy.

Athletics was another way to stand out. I played most sports, only slightly sucking at baseball. I was pretty good at everything, but not outstanding at anything. Good enough to make all the teams and play, but not the star. I really wanted to be the star. I could lead, but I wasn't blessed with outstanding athletic skill. But people would follow me. I was blessed with speed and a great motor—a *want to* that enabled me to outwork and outwit many I came up against. And my German heritage gave me a stubbornness that allowed me to compete.

Trophies were how I measured myself. And I wanted them. Badly. So I gave it all I had all the time. I played hard. I practiced hard. I didn't stop. We didn't get trophies for showing up like later generations. We earned them. And if you didn't earn them, you were weak. No way

I was going to be called weak. So I toiled and toiled, until one day I won a championship. It was in soccer. I was in the sixth grade. I played center forward and didn't score the most goals, but I scored plenty. Finally, I was content. Sort of. For a while. Until the next season. The next sport. The next schoolyard game. I had to win. I had to kick *your* ass. When I was on the field or court or track, I hated you. I hated whoever was in between me and the trophy. I ended up winning lots of trophies. Trophies in all the sports I played. It felt so good to win, and I was always chasing that "winning buzz." Unfortunately, chasing buzzes would become a common theme for me.

I was a crappy loser too. The refs always sucked. The foul was never on me. Your parents were jerks. The other teams were the enemy and had to be destroyed. If I sound like a jackass, I pretty much was. I loved my family and my friends and teammates, but my dial was pretty much set to win and destroy. Except for schoolwork. That was a bunch of crap I didn't need to know. Because I already knew everything. And if you questioned me or challenged me, I would blow up.

But I was also pretty darn charming, good at getting what I wanted. And funny. Really funny. I feared no teacher or coach. If I made you laugh, you would like me, and I would feel a part of something. That helped me a lot in life. So did my uber-competitive nature. Man, did it help me. I wouldn't know how much it would help until later in life. Much later. When I learned that God doesn't give you anything you can't handle. He gives you all the tools you need to make it through life.

I had a lot to learn, so I had to go through a lot of pain.

As a child, however, I had no real relationship with God. I only went to church because my parents made me. I never listened or wanted to be there. In fact, I felt so uncomfortable at church that I literally ran outside and threw up several times. I suppose I never much liked being told what to do. This worked against me quite a bit. It took me losing almost everything I had, at least the most important stuff like my wife and kids, before I was ever able to accept God and His will for me. Pain is a great teacher. Most times the only teacher I could learn from. I had a lot to learn, so I had to go through a lot of pain.

And did I ever on September 24, 2016.

I woke up that Saturday morning with a plan to do what I always do. Work out, then head to my weekly fellowship meeting. But that morning was a little different. I had just returned from a weeklong business trip to London. Although the primary reason I was there was to make sales calls, I had managed to inquire about a half marathon in Kew Gardens—the Richmond Half. It's a very popular race, one you need to register early for, as it sells out quickly. But with only two months until the race, it was already full. The only way to gain entry was to enter as a fundraiser for charity, which seemed like a cool thing to do. So with my mom recently requiring round-the-clock care in a skilled nursing facility in my hometown of Louisville, it made sense that I chose to raise money for Alzheimer's. In fact, I ended up the number two fundraiser and made a donation of over $4,500. Talk about gratifying.

The race and countryside were as beautiful as advertised—a lovely park run for the first couple miles followed by many miles along a tow road that paralleled the Thames, ending in Richmond Park. It was great fun, with a festival at the finish. I spent some time postrace wandering around Richmond Park, taking it all in.

But the next morning I awoke to a really sore right hamstring. The same one that has bothered me since I ran the New York City Marathon in 2015—a little celebration for turning fifty years old—and a challenge to myself. I decided that if I was ever going to run a marathon, I needed to get it done. And being the egomaniac that I am, naturally I had to run the biggest one.

So I called a friend of mine, Kelly Fillnow, who is a world-class triathlete and a coach. I told her that I not only wanted to run the New York Marathon but also get my time under three hours and thirty minutes, so I could qualify for the big daddy: Boston. And then I was going to hang it up.

She got me into the best shape of my life in the three months leading up to the New York City Marathon. I had zero injuries. There were no hiccups. I did every single thing she told me to do to the letter. It's amazing what happens when you follow instructions. I came into that race rock solid. I had run a twenty-three-mile stint three weeks out, a couple of twenty-mile stints, and a couple of eighteen-mile stretches as well. Man, was I ready.

Based upon my times, I figured I was going to run about a three-hour-and-twenty-three-minute race in New York ... which would have qualified me for the Boston Marathon easily. But it happened to be 60°F at the start on November 1 in Manhattan. It's never that warm. In fact, it was 70°F in Central Park when we finished. I'm of German heritage, so my body prefers the cold. I ended up running a great race, but the heat slowed me and lots of other runners down a little bit at the end. I missed the Boston Marathon qualifying time by five minutes.

It was a few weeks after that when I started having a nagging hamstring injury, pretty much a chronic deal. Basically, my gluteus muscles just weren't firing properly on my right side, forcing my hamstring to do all the work, getting inflamed and hurting like hell after a hard effort.

Kelly and I tried just about everything to fix it. First, we tried Active Release Technique, which is a combination of movement with specific pressure points around the injury to release the muscle and tendons from being all jacked up. Then, we tried TENS, stretching, strengthening, acupuncture, and even a cortisone injection … *no bueno*. The only thing we didn't try was rest. Imagine that. So after the half marathon in London, Kelly told me I needed to take a month off and only bike and swim … no running at all. I reluctantly agreed.

Funny thing about the bike. I never really wanted to buy one. Bikers get hit by cars all the time in Charlotte. Don't get me wrong—I enjoy the bike. I love the speed and the wind moving across my body, the struggle and the feeling of accomplishment after a hard bout of biking. But I feared what *could* happen. Most of my bike rides would be on streets with bike lanes … the few streets in Charlotte that have them, that is. But like anything else, I got bored with the same routes and gained enough confidence to set out on a route that didn't have designated bike lanes.

Saturday morning, the plan was an hour-long ride along a loop I had ridden many times. The difference this time was in both time of day and conditions. It was late September, and we were coming up on the time change. Fall back. So at 6:20 in the morning, it was still dark. First light was close behind, but with the leaves on the trees and the heavy tree canopy of Charlotte, it was really dark.

I also had a couple other things working against me that morning. It was super humid. The dew point was in the mid-70s, and the air was heavy … so much so that I could feel the dampness on my handlebars just a few minutes into the ride. It was also a new moon, so combined with the sun not quite beginning to backlight the sky, there was no moonlight at all.

Never one to worry about a few extra things to overcome, I geared up like any geeky dad would. Helmet, light on the back of my bike, reflective socks, and even a vest with reflectors and flashing LED lights.

It wasn't quite like 30 Rock in New York City on Christmas, but in the dark with lights on, it's actually easier to see something than in the middle of the day when you can get camouflaged by all the other things going on around you. I felt like it would only be a few minutes until light anyway, so I set out.

It's about a mile from my house on Silver Bell Drive to Sharon Lane, due north. As I pedaled up the hill, the heavy air was on me and on my handlebars … I felt it all over my body. When approaching Sharon Lane, a boulevard separates the road. It's comprised of cedar trees and grass, and you could smell that distinct and comforting smell of cedar wood. My front wheel hit a couple small potholes—holes I couldn't quite see in the darkness—and it jarred my body. No streetlights yet. At that point I thought it might be best that I turn around, so I did. But just for a few yards. I went back to where the boulevard divided the road and said to myself, "Come on, Dean, just get it done." So I turned back north and headed out of the neighborhood. Note to self: trust your gut. It's almost always right.

Note to self: trust your gut. It's almost always right.

I took a right on Sharon Lane, reassured with the safety of the streetlights. I could now see better and rode the half mile to Providence Road. Incidentally, *Providence* means "under the care of God." At Providence, the light was red to turn left, but at the early hour, not a car was in sight. So I turned left and headed north toward Uptown Charlotte.

As I began my ride northward, I picked up quite a bit of speed quickly, given that I was riding slightly downhill. Not thirty seconds later, I was traveling over twenty-three miles per hour, and three cars came flying by me on my left. Providence Road is also North Carolina Route 16, a state-maintained road and one heavily traveled. But at

6:30 on Saturday morning, those were the first cars I encountered in either direction. It's also four lanes, boulevard divided, and I was riding in the middle of the right lane. So I was doing everything right, at least that's what I thought when these cars that appeared to be racing came flying by. I looked to my left and thought, *Why the heck are those guys in such a hurry?*

Just as I refocused myself and looked straight ahead, I heard a terrible sound: wheels locking up behind me. I thought, *This guy is losing the race, and he's recklessly trying to catch up with the three cars that just passed me. How can he not see me? What the heck is he thinking? Is he texting and driving?*

About the time that last thought left my head, I felt the impact. I heard the tires lock up, rubber wailing, my own rear tire and wheel exploding, and then … silence.

Upon awakening, I could hear faint siren sounds, growing louder. Two young guys stood over me. One started to pick my bike up to move it. Even with the force of a Ford F-150 truck traveling at 45 mph, my feet managed to stay clipped in. My hands rested near my handlebars, bloodied. My Day-Glo-yellow bike jersey was torn to pieces, my left shoulder shredded. I could feel the blood on my left cheek as I came to, my face laying on the asphalt.

I stopped him and said, "Leave the bike alone. Don't move it, and don't move me! I can't feel anything below my waist. I can't move my legs. I think I'm paralyzed."

They told me to stay still, that they had called 9-1-1. The sirens were getting louder. My initial reaction? I was totally pissed! How did they not see me? I was lit up like a Christmas tree! I did everything right. Had all the gear on. Rode in the right lane. Had a light, had a vest with lights. Had reflective socks. Dammit, how did they not see me?

Then I asked them myself, "Guys, how did you not see me?"

The driver of the truck spoke up first. "It's really dark, and the condensation on my windshield made it hard to see. I didn't see you until I was fifteen or twenty feet from you, and as soon as I did, I slammed on the brakes. But I knew it was too late, and I knew I was going to hit you. I'm so sorry."

I looked up at him. And then I did what I always do when I meet someone for the first time. I said, "Hey, I'm Dean. What are your names?"

"My name is Will," said the driver. "And this is my friend, Andre."

Then the training kicked in, and I knew what to do. When I got sober seven years earlier, I learned some things that not only keep you sober but also keep you sane. Right-sized. In the moment. And in that moment I did what I knew I had to do. It wasn't a chore. It was instinct. I really didn't even think about it. I just did it. I began to pray.

At that moment, I prayed: "God, I have no idea what you have in store for me. I know that your plan for me is beyond any human comprehension. I just ask that you take care of my family and you give the doctors the wisdom and skill to put me back together and to serve you."

In that moment, I also forgave the driver, Will, this man who I had never met. A man who ran me over with his truck. I had to forgive Will, because resentment is the evil seed that makes us crazy, steals our serenity. It steals our sobriety. It takes our energy and turns it against us.

Through God's plan, Will crossed my path, and God had a plan for both of us. And then I was at peace. I had no fear. I had God's love. When you have God's love, there is no fear.

God had this, and I had to trust that.

CHAPTER TWO:

THE VILLAIN

When something bad happens, we usually assume there's a good guy and a villain. But sometimes bad things happen to good people on both sides. In an accident like mine, it's easy to jump to conclusions—the guy must have been drunk. Or high. Or both. It was probably a criminal fleeing the police. Or a self-centered moron who was posting on Facebook when he should have been watching the road.

> **I couldn't have been run down by a nicer guy.**

I can definitely say, in my case, I couldn't have been run down by a nicer guy.

Will Huffman grew up in Lynchburg, Virginia, the only child of parents who taught at Virginia Episcopal School (VES), one of the most well-respected boarding schools in the state. Will's parents not only worked there, but the family actually lived on campus for much of Will's childhood. To say VES had a big impact on who Will Huffman is would be an understatement. You spend your first eighteen years of life anywhere, and it's bound to make an impact. But don't think that because Will's folks were faculty members that he took advantage of the situation. I probably would have milked that opportunity. Not Will. He worked just as hard and studied just as hard as his classmates.

His father was a coach and into sports big-time. But that really wasn't Will's passion, so he knew early on that he needed to make his own way in life. Soon, Will discovered that *leadership* was more his thing. He joined and led many student organizations, including being the senior captain of his cross-country team—even though running wasn't exactly his strong suit. But that's part of what makes someone a leader. They're not always the most skilled person. It's their ability to bring out the best in others that matters.

Will's proficiency in leadership came to fruition when he was elected by his peers to be the Chair of the Honor Committee. This long-standing body was created for students to uphold the school's honor code, which was basically a list of what *not* to do—don't lie, don't cheat others, don't steal. But Will didn't stop there. He decided to take that a step further and add something to the honor code—making it also about being *proactive* in doing the right things. So Will founded Honor and Integrity Week at VES during his senior year.

He reached out to a bunch of different colleges in the areas— UNC Chapel Hill, UVA, Davidson—and recruited representatives to come in and speak at the inaugural event. Not long ago, Will's parents were going through boxes tucked away in their basement and found a letter written to Will from one of those first speakers. He was from Washington and Lee University and wanted Will to know what an honor it had been to be invited to VES for such an important occasion.

Upon Will's graduation, he won the Chaplain's Prize—an award chosen by the school chaplain for the person who best carries out the mission of the school. In the years since, Honor and Integrity Week has grown immensely and become a tradition. And not just at Will's alma mater, but at all the colleges where Will and those who came after him recruited speakers. Will did so much more than build an extracurricular activity. He built a legacy.

See what I mean about Will Huffman? Talk about a strong compass and good heart. Even in middle school he won a local citizenship award that came with a scholarship. If anyone has ever been born an old soul, it's Will Huffman.

Family, faith, and his school's culture obviously played a huge role in who Will is. He grew up attending Peakland Baptist Church and was a leader in the youth ministry. He spent his summers working in hot, sweaty warehouses for a couple shoe distribution companies. For Will, it was a summer job. For his coworkers, it was their livelihood. Will's grandfather spent almost his entire life in a similar line of work. He always taught Will that everyone deserved the same level of respect, regardless of their position. And by treating his coworkers that way, they became Will's friends. He learned so many lessons he says he carries with him to this day from them—like how to pool money together when someone needed flowers or a meal. How to win concert tickets through radio contests, regardless of whether you liked the band or not. Because even if you didn't, you could give the tickets to someone who did.

But there is someone else who had a major impact on Will's heart. An unlikely friend, one decades older, who Will met when he was about seven years old.

Across the street from VES was a fairly affluent retirement community. And sometimes when Will was out riding his bike, he would be drawn in that direction when the occasional EMS vehicle was called. It was on one of those days that young Will jumped on his bike and rode over to see what all the commotion was about when he came across Sam Williams—a retired banker in his midseventies. Sam was checking out what was going on as well, and the two struck up a conversation. Not long after that the two became fast friends. In fact, Will's family and Sam and his wife, Helen, often spent time together.

Sam and Helen had no children of their own, so the older man took a sincere interest in Will as he grew up—in his studies and ambitions. And then one night during Will's senior year, Sam was over for dinner and stunned everyone.

"So where are you planning on going after graduation?" Sam asked.

Sam had gone to the rival University of Virginia, but Will had to break the news. It was all in good spirits though. "I landed on Virginia Tech."

"Well, I'm going to pay for you to go to college."

And that's exactly what Sam Williams did. Will would come home from Virginia Tech occasionally and share with Sam how he was doing. Then, just two weeks before Will graduated in 2012, his dear friend and mentor passed away. But Will knows Sam was there, in the audience, cheering him on just the same. It was a strong friendship that shaped Will's sense of paying it forward, giving back, and helping others. After Sam's death, even more stories of humble giving emerged—$100,000 given to one organization, $100,000 for another. And another. And another. All the while Sam drove the same old Volkswagen Quantum station wagon until the very end.

A true leader at heart, Will had been the president of his business fraternity at Virginia Tech. Understandably, he had made a lot of business connections in that role that served him well. Shortly after Will graduated, he was recruited by Otis and moved to Charlotte to start a career in sales.

Will didn't know a soul in Charlotte. But he'd never lived anywhere other than Virginia, so he was excited to get out into the world. Charlotte is a relatively big city, so Will thought it was pretty cool to live in a place that had its own professional sports teams and public transit. Those first couple of years were a lot of fun. He met some great friends. And eventually he met Jeanelle, the woman who would become his wife.

Jeanelle was from Wisconsin originally. Her sister had been living in Charlotte, so when Jeanelle graduated she moved south to become a teacher. At the time, Will happened to be the leader of a small church group that met at his condo each week. The way the online platform on the church's website worked, it allowed people to search for a group that would be conveniently located. As luck would have it, Will's condo was about a half mile from the school where Jeanelle taught. So she signed up for Will's group, and the rest is history. They became fast friends. Then they became more than friends. And in October of 2015, they were married.

It was about a month shy of their one-year anniversary when our two worlds collided—literally.

A couple days prior to the accident, Will's good friend, Andre, had come to Charlotte. Andre is one of those carefree adventure-seekers who enjoys wandering the world and wondering at it. He called Will out of the blue one day and suggested he fly into town so the two could hit the Virginia Tech game on Saturday. Otherwise, Will would have never been on the road that morning.

The plan was right after the game, Will would drop Andre off at Roanoke-Blacksburg Regional Airport near the college instead of driving him back to Charlotte. So after a couple of days together, the buddies rose early Saturday morning to make the three-hour drive from Charlotte to Virginia Tech.

Neither one of us will ever forget how dark and foggy it was that morning. Will has always considered himself a careful driver. Not so much as a speeding ticket. The kind of driver that keeps in the right lane unless he has to pass. Which was the lane I was riding my bike in just ahead.

Will doesn't remember being passed by the cars racing by. Trauma does that. It steals your memory. He does, however, remember having both hands on the wheel. He couldn't make out much ahead of him. He never saw the lights on my bike. He never saw my reflective socks.

By the time Will saw me, it was too late. He knew there was nothing he could do.

He slammed on the brakes. "Holy shit! Fuck!"

The tires squealed. His heavy, gray F-150 rammed hard into my back bike tire. He says he barely felt a thing. Just a dull thud. I went flying. Will slowed to a stop. The car traveling behind Will's truck stopped and called 9-1-1. Will threw the truck in park and sprang into action. He and Andre were kneeling over me, asking if I was all right. Will was super shaken up.

"Guys, how did you not see me?" I asked.

Trembling, Will answered. "It's really dark … and the condensation on my windshield made it hard to see. I didn't see you until I was fifteen or twenty feet from you. As soon as I did, I slammed on the brakes. But I knew it was too late. I knew I was going to hit you. I'm so sorry."

Right away I knew he was telling the truth. "Hey, I'm Dean. What are your names?"

Will was surprised the medics got there so quickly. So was I. Grateful as hell too. There was a huge police presence due to recent riots, racial protests, and unrest in Charlotte following the police shooting of Keith Lamont Scott, so cops were everywhere that particular morning. As soon as they showed up, they were obviously very worried about me. Will was worried about me too. But one officer in particular was worried about Will. He wanted to make sure the young man involved in this terrible accident was okay. He told Will this kind of thing happened more often than people realized. That didn't really make Will feel better in the moment, but it did make him feel a little bit less of a villain.

The thing is: no one on the scene really knew the extent of the damage to my spine. I mean, I was talking, coherent, answering questions. We all knew it was a back injury, but that's about it. So Will and Andre waited around anxiously while I was loaded onto a stretcher and into the ambulance. Will had given all of his information to the police. And because I was the one laying in the road, he received a citation. Will didn't do anything wrong, so the cop didn't really know what to write him up for. The citation ended up reading something like: "Following Too Closely." No fine. No court appearance. And then, that was it. The accident scene was cleared. For Will, it was all over.

Except it wasn't. Because that's the kind of guy Will Huffman is.

He was so distraught he couldn't drive. He had Andre take the wheel. Will would have gladly turned right around and gone home to his wife, but Andre had a flight out of Roanoke later that evening so they couldn't turn back. Will's mind was on Dean the rest of the drive to Virginia Tech. He tried to call Jeanelle, but she was still asleep. It wasn't even 7:00 a.m. by that point. He sent her a message: "Please call me back."

Jeanelle eventually did call Will back. He barely got the words out. "I hit a bicyclist. I … don't know any other way to say it."

"Is he hurt? How bad is it?"

"It's pretty bad. I don't know his last name. I don't know his condition. I don't know anything."

Imagine trying to move on with your life knowing what you were just involved in. Never hearing the rest of the story. Will went with

Andre to the Virginia Tech game. He was haunted the whole time. Even if he went back home, what could he do? He was emotionally paralyzed, just sitting there.

And it was that way for Will for nearly a week. He could barely function. He'd get up. He'd go to work. He'd go home. He'd crawl in bed. The founder of the Honor and Integrity Week at Virginia Episcopal School needed closure. He needed to see the man he had hit.

And all he knew was my first name.

CHAPTER THREE:

THE ROCK

Beth was awakened by the worst call a loved one can possibly receive. Remember, this was a Saturday morning—early. Any other Saturday morning and I'd have gotten my run in early—like starting at 5:30 or 6:00 a.m.—then headed out to my men's fellowship meeting at 8:00 a.m., before anyone was out of bed. Hell, I shouldn't have even been on that bike. I should have been running with my buddy, Tony, at McAlpine Park.

But this wasn't any other Saturday morning. I was laying there, literally broken in half on Providence Road. Cops and EMTs swarming everywhere. My wife had no clue anything was wrong.

I tried to be as calm as possible. I asked the policeman to get the phone out of the back pocket of my cycling jersey so I could call Beth.

I dialed. "Honey?"

"Yeah?" she replied, her voice dreamy.

Later, Beth told me she thought I was still in London when I called. She wondered why the heck I had forgotten about the time difference. Then she remembered. I had flown home Friday afternoon.

We had dinner together. The jet lag had me exhausted, so I crashed early and told her I was going for a bike ride instead of running in the morning.

From that moment on, she says she remembers every single detail that happened. Every bit of the next twenty-four hours. "More vividly than childbirth," she tells me.

"I've been hit. I'm on Providence Road. I was riding my bike, and somebody hit me from behind."

"Dean, are you okay?"

"Yeah, I think so—" Which was total bullshit. I knew something was wrong, but I didn't want to scare her.

She was obviously concerned, but at that point she was thinking I had a broken arm. Maybe a broken leg. A police officer took the phone from me at that moment, literally midsentence. I had gone into shock and wasn't making any sense. He introduced himself to Beth, then said: "I'm here with your husband. The ambulance is on the way. He's been hit by a truck."

Because Providence Road is about three minutes away, Beth leapt up. "Wait! I'll be right there. I want to ride to the hospital with him. I'll just throw some clothes on—"

"Ma'am, we don't have time for that," he told her. "Just meet us at the hospital."

Beth didn't meet the police at the hospital, however. She *beat* them there. That's Beth. She's my rock. She'd been there for me in some of my darkest hours. I'll get to that later. I wasn't always the easiest guy to live with. And Beth's early life was no cakewalk either.

She was born in Columbus, Mississippi, to Sue Garrard, who had recently graduated high school and was looking forward to starting college in the fall. Beth's mother was from a good family—well respected in the community. Beth's father ... well, not so much. He was the bad boy, always in fights. The football star with a full scholarship to play football at Mississippi State.

When Beth's parents found out they were pregnant in the summer of 1966, Beth's grandfather, Otis Garrard, begged Sue not to marry him. But she did. Beth's dad turned down the scholarship to Mississippi State to play football, and both her parents ended up enrolling in Mississippi State University. They only lasted about eight months together.

Beth's father was extremely abusive, both mentally and physically. He was an alcoholic as well, even at such a young age. So after her mother and father broke it off, Beth and her mom ended up moving back to Columbus. Beth's grandparents' housekeeper, Alberta, took care of Beth while Sue, her mother, went to Mississippi University for Women. Eventually, Beth's mother moved with her to Jackson and enrolled at Millsaps College for her final classes. Kind and supportive as they were, Beth's grandparents paid for a housekeeper to keep an eye on Beth while her mother finished her education.

When Beth was about four years old, her mother met a man and fell in love. The two got married, had two sons, and they all lived as a family for eight years. But he was an alcoholic too. And Beth's mother eventually had enough. Sue is super smart, an extremely hard worker, and uber competent. People just love her. So with three kids and two failed marriages, Beth's mother moved to Memphis, Tennessee. She'd been transferred there through her job at a brokerage firm, and as she began working her way up the corporate ladder she began traveling for work extensively.

Atlanta was where Beth and her family landed next. Her mom worked her way up the corporate ladder, shattering glass ceilings in the finance industry as she went. When Beth was in ninth grade, her mother finally found her soulmate—a coworker named Bill who eventually became Beth's stepfather.

Bill was immediately adored by everyone. An amazing guy. Funny, loves sports, a former Marine—a man's man. At last Beth had a father figure she could love and count on—aside from her grandfather, that is. Throughout those early years, Beth always looked at her grandfather as a father figure. She remained very close to both her grandparents, oftentimes spending whole summers with them. But, by then, Beth and her mother had a very tumultuous relationship. So many moves, so much traveling for work takes its toll on a child.

When they lived in Memphis, Beth's grandparents had paid for her to attend a private, all-girls Catholic school. Great school. Great education. Not such a great experience for Beth. The majority of the girls who attended came from old Mississippi money. The carpool lane was filled with Mercedes station wagons and moms who had been out playing tennis all day. It was intimidating. She felt like Cinderella, always comparing herself to the other girls. The things they had. The opportunities they had. The mom they had.

So understandably Beth was angry. She was resentful that her mother couldn't be like the other mothers. Of course, Beth wasn't old enough to appreciate the hard work and sacrifices her mother was making at the time. She was doing her best. Life wasn't easy for any of them.

Things eventually reached a breaking point when Beth's mom started traveling to New York from Georgia more and more often. Beth started to rebel. So at the beginning of Beth's tenth-grade year, her grandfather came into town and with her mom and Bill brought her to an all-girls boarding school against her will. This made Beth hate her mother even more. Go figure. She rode that out for six months until finally Beth's grandparents brought her home to live with them until her mother stopped traveling so much.

Beth's reaction? She loved it. That was exactly the kind of life and the kind of love Beth needed to heal her soul. For the first time in her young life, she had a mom figure at home who would make her lunch every day, who would be waiting with cookies when Beth got home from school. So Beth just kept on living with them until she graduated high school.

She went on to get a degree in banking and finance at Mississippi State and ended up working as a sales assistant at a brokerage herself. It was a great job but didn't pay very well starting off at the ground level, so Beth took a job as a hostess and server at The Public House on Roswell Square, a fine-dining restaurant nearby. The very restaurant where yours truly was working as a server and wait-staff trainer.

I was going to Georgia State at the time—you know the drill—school by day, work by night. Every night at the restaurant we had a lineup. We had to make sure everyone's uniforms were pressed, the handwritten menu chalkboards were right, the tables were set, and the silver and glasses were polished. We were all hanging out at the bottom of this beautiful, grand staircase going through which stations each waiter was going to be assigned to. Well, I looked up at the top of the stairs, and who did I see? This beautiful SEC princess, as my waiter buddies called her ... as in the South East Conference, where Kentucky, Alabama, Georgia, Mississippi State, and others compete. She was and is a knockout, and well, let's just say it was game over. Love at first sight. At least that's how Beth describes it. Okay, I fell in love right away too. She maintains that very night she told her best friend she'd just met the man she was going to marry. Did I mention how smart Beth is? Anyway, we started dating shortly after that first meeting, and we've been inseparable from that moment on. Through the good and the bad.

And as Beth raced to the hospital to face more of the bad, all she kept wondering was: *How bad?* The police pulled in right behind her and parked in a designated spot. Beth circled the lot, looking for an opening. Then she decided, *screw it*, and spun into a handicap spot. To hell with a parking ticket when her husband has just been rushed to the hospital.

On her way into the emergency room, she spotted my bike in the back of the police officer's car, the back tire blown out and mangled. The safety light still flashing red. It's never a good sign when you go into the ER as a visitor, and they don't even mess with signing you in. Once the triage staff knew Beth was there to see me, they just ushered her back to the little room I was laying in.

The first thing she saw when she pulled the curtain back was me in a hospital gown, hooked to IVs, snapping selfies for Facebook. She wasn't too happy about that under the circumstances. In my defense, I was given a high dose of morphine two minutes before she walked in. The ambulance ride was excruciating. I never had—and God willing never will experience again—that level of pain.

After she got me to put the phone down, she asked, "Are you okay?"

"I can't feel anything from the waist down."

She took her finger and rubbed it across my legs, my thigh, my toe. "Nothing?"

"No."

Then she ran her finger on the outside of my right foot.

"I kind of feel that," I said.

Neither of us knew anything was seriously wrong with my back at that point. It was the furthest thing from our minds that I could be permanently paralyzed. In fact, we were just talking and joking around when two of my running buddies showed up—Zack and Tony. I was supposed to meet up with them after my ride, so Beth called to let them know I wasn't going to make it. Both superathletes. Both superhuman beings. My good friend, Drew, even showed up, which is really saying something about how lucky I am to be surrounded by such amazing people. This guy hated hospitals with a passion because he'd been in them so often battling ulcerative colitis.

Within a few minutes the tiny room was flooded with friends laughing and nurses taking vitals. They wouldn't tell us anything other than they were going to wheel me down for an MRI, and that they had informed the ER neurologist of the situation and called in a neurosurgeon. Before I left, Beth and my friends all linked hands and prayed over me.

I felt their love. I felt God's love. And off I went.

Sometimes, there are just no words for the gratitude you feel.

While I was getting my MRI, Tony kept Beth company. He was the rock for *my* rock, making sure she was comfortable. Making sure she had coffee. Making sure she had something in her stomach. How do you properly thank someone for something like that? You can't. I've tried. Sometimes, there are just no words for the gratitude you feel.

About twenty minutes later, I was wheeled back into the room. Within minutes the ER neurologist came in with the preliminary results. Tony stepped outside.

The doctor walked around the right side of my bed. "There's a lot of damage. We need to get you to surgery immediately because there's no blood supply to your spine right now. Time is critical. I've paged one of my partners, the neurosurgeon on call. His name is Matt McGirt."

In case you haven't noticed, I don't do BS. I want to look something right in the eyes and deal with it head on.

"Don't bullshit me," I said. "I need to know the real deal."

He stared back at me without emotion. "Dean, it's not good."

For whatever reason, I was at peace at that point. Concerned, but not fearful. I had given it over to God. Whatever was going to happen was out of my hands. The neurologist left with Beth trailing close behind.

She stopped him in the hall. "What do you mean, it's not good? You need to tell me what's going on."

"Beth, his back is fractured in half," he said. "He has vertebrae that are going to need to be rebuilt."

Then Beth asked the very question I was asking God: "Is he going to walk again?"

"I don't know," he replied. "But it's not looking very promising."

Beth says she nearly threw up in the hall at that moment. A million things were running through her mind. *But he's so active? What does this mean for the rest of his life?*

In less than ten minutes, the neurologist returned and told us the surgeon had arrived and was getting ready to operate. Beth and I held each other. We kissed. We all prayed. Beth, Tony, Drew, Zach, and I. Then they wheeled me away to prep for surgery.

It was approaching 8:00 a.m. when the neurologist directed Beth and Tony to a waiting room on floor three of the hospital. There, Beth called one of her closest friends, Becca. She told her what had happened and asked her to head to our house to be there when our fourteen-year-old daughter, Grace, woke up. Beth asked Becca not to arouse any suspicion as to anything being wrong. She just wanted Grace to have a familiar face to wake up to.

Beth called her mom and stepdad. They said they were hopping in the car immediately and would be there in an hour and ten minutes. Then she called Caroline Wilson, a really good, old friend, reaching back to our newlywed days in Atlanta, who is also really good in a crisis. Caroline happened to be in the car with her husband. She said she was on her way to the hospital and needed to make a quick call to Dr. Dwyer, a trusted friend of hers … and coincidentally one of Matt McGirt's partners. A few minutes later, Caroline called Beth back.

"Beth, Dr. Dwyer was already briefed about Dean," she said. "He said Dean is lucky Matt was on call this morning. If it had been him, he wouldn't have taken on Dean's surgery. He would have called Matt. He's the best neurosurgeon on the East Coast. This is his specialty. This is what he does best."

I was in God's hands. And I was in Matt's.

CHAPTER FOUR:

THE OUTLIER

Matt McGirt is an outlier. He's one of the most, if not *the* most, published medical professionals in Charlotte. He's an academic and an innovator. He's the kind of doctor that you'd normally think of leading the faculty at Duke University or Johns Hopkins University, writing papers only the best of the best would even comprehend. The Stephen Hawking of neurosurgery.

Instead, Matt chose to return to his hometown of Charlotte to practice medicine. For the uninitiated, Charlotte is a nonmedical-school, nonacademic community when compared to cities with a Duke or Johns Hopkins. But it has a very progressive medical center that excels in trauma care. And thankfully, of all the hospitals and medical facilities in the world, Matt happened to be in Charlotte and on call the morning of my accident.

The fact is Matt McGirt has been an outlier his whole life. Seriously, what kid loves going to the doctor's office? Matt McGirt did. Endless doctor visits for allergy shots for seven years? Loved it. Watching friends get stitches in a gaping wound? Couldn't get enough.

It's not like there was a long line of doctors in the family either. His dad was a lawyer.

Matt was even an outlier in his own family. Having been raised by Carolina Tarheels, he ended up going to Duke, a top-three university that year. He never tested great on standardized tests but was an overachiever based on work ethic. He could outwork *anybody*. Sounds familiar. Finishing at the top of his class at an elite school is incredibly relevant to landing specialties like neurosurgery.

Matt knew he wanted to be a surgeon as soon as he got to med school. High-pressure, split decisions, quick interventions, quick results—that was Matt. And when he did his medical school rotations, he realized he loved the nervous system and brain. So neurosurgery was the perfect combination to live his passions.

The chances of my path crossing with Matt's that early Saturday morning in Charlotte were astronomical.

Matt also realized as a medical student that he had a special talent with data and analytics. So while still in medical school, he began independently publishing his own work. By the time he finished Duke Med, Matt had published more articles than any four-year medical student *ever*—something like forty independent, peer-reviewed, national publications.

It was that kind of overachieving that helped him land his residency at Johns Hopkins, the birthplace of neurosurgery. Just to put into perspective how elite Matt's neurosurgery skills are, we're talking about a school that only accepts three people each year out of *all the applicants in the world*. See what I mean? The chances of my path crossing with Matt's that early Saturday morning in Charlotte were astronomical.

But like all paths, they don't come without a few bumps and detours. And Matt certainly had his share.

He spent his first seven years practicing in Baltimore with his bride, Laura, at his side. Who he happened to meet at med school. Who also happened to be valedictorian of their class—the number one female student that year, and number two overall. The couple had three children during their respective residencies at Johns Hopkins. While working one-hundred-hour weeks. They would meet at gas stations in between shifts to hand the kids off to each other.

It was during years five through seven that Matt solidified his love for spine surgery. It was the perfect balance of nerve work, soft tissue work, bone work, and reconstruction with metal and rods. He had the amazing good fortune to work alongside one of the preeminent spine surgeons on the planet, Ziya Gokaslan, and so was exposed to the biggest, most challenging, most amazing spine surgeries ever performed. For perspective, surgeons would come from around the world to watch these complicated surgeries.

By the time Matt got to his Chief Residency year, he had over 150 independent scientific peer-reviewed publications. Statistically, we're talking about the top one percentile. In fact, Matt McGirt was the most published resident ever to graduate from the number one neurosurgery program in the country. And so he went on to an academic job at Vanderbilt University, joining the faculty of the School of Medicine. Laura joined the Department of Dermatology.

As the complex-spine surgeon for the entire Vanderbilt University Medical Center, within three years Matt had become the number one producer for the entire healthcare system. That just means he did a ton of cases. And that's because there was a great need in the Deep South. All five states surrounding Tennessee would ship any and every complicated spine problem right to Vanderbilt.

Matt was in heaven. He got to do some of his most challenging spine cases during those first three years of his career. He continued to publish. He founded the National Registry for Spinal Injuries. His office was decorated with every single award in neurosurgery you could possibly win. Something he used to call his "I Love Me" wall. Needless to say, his parents were proud. Matt was poised to take over the directorship for the spine division across Vanderbilt University in just his fourth year.

He was an outlier. An overachiever. Matt was one of the highest-paid people in the entire hospital system—making more than anyone in the legal department, in administration, on the medical staff, you name it—just based on the sheer volume of patients he served. Hell, he even had the producers of the television show *Grey's Anatomy* write an episode based on the miraculous success story of one of his operations—a woman who had been practically decapitated and needed her head reattached to her neck and spine!

With all the success, the praise, the papers, and the patients, Matt McGirt could have soared as high as he dreamed. But dreams like that come with a cost. A cost Matt realized he wasn't willing to pay. So he reflected. He shifted his priorities. And he chose family over a career. He found balance.

Matt realized that life was not about his medical innovations or how awesome his surgery skills were or how many awards he could collect. Life is about relationships. It's about our connection with humanity. He wanted to connect with the human side of his skills, grateful and blessed to be able simply to use his talents to help other human beings. So he decided he was going back to his hometown to join the preeminent private practice neurosurgery group in Charlotte.

Actually, Matt became part of the largest neurosurgery group in the world. All the surgeons participated in something called

E-Service—the letter "E" standing for *emergency*. This is a way for everyone to maintain their practices during the days, as long as they commit to three weeks each year to serve at the local trauma center.

So as I was being rushed to the ER that Saturday morning, feeling like a thousand daggers were being plunged into my back, Matt had just arrived for day one of his seven-day shift. It's crazy to think of all the blessings that had to align that morning. The police arrived at the scene of the accident within sixty seconds. The ambulance was there in four and a half minutes. Carolinas Medical Center, the busiest level-one trauma center in the state, was a mile away. And arguably one of the best neurosurgeons in the world with a core competency in exactly my injury just happened to be working one of his three Saturdays of the year.

Matt arrived at 7:00 a.m. I arrived at 7:01. He was just about to run the list of rounds when his resident got the call about me being in the ER. Now just a side note here: for whatever reason, the ER was not busy. In fact, it was unusually slow. If you've ever been to an emergency room, you know that they typically check you in. You go through triage to make sure you're not dying. No heart attack? No blood gushing? Have a seat and wait your turn. Even with a spinal injury, if you can't move your legs they call for a neurosurgery consultation. They get a CT scan. They get X-rays. Twenty minutes here. Ten minutes there. That's not how my visit went at all. Thank God, because I didn't know it then, but I didn't have that kind of time.

Matt told the resident to head down to the ER to check me out instead of waiting for the CT scan. He gave me morphine right away. He asked if I could move my legs. I couldn't. He pulled out a safety pin and straightened it. He poked and prodded up and down my legs with the sharp end. Nothing. He tried the rounded end. Nothing. He grabbed a Q-tip and brushed it against my skin. A very slight sensation along my right foot. Nothing else below my belly button. He then left.

A CT scan was ordered immediately. Matt waited by his computer and watched as it came up on his screen. Before it was even finished loading, he knew I was in trouble. My spine was snapped in two. And dislocated. I had some sensation, but I couldn't move my legs at all.

Spinal injuries are graded by the American Spinal Injury Association (ASIA) as ASIA A, B, C, or D. ASIA A means there's no sensory and no motor function—complete paralysis. At that point, the spinal cord is likely severed or too damaged to be able to do anything meaningful. With ASIA A, time doesn't matter. ASIA B, on the other hand, means there is no motor function, but the patient can still feel a little bit. So technically, some signal is getting through. Which means hope. Which means time is critical.

Matt determined that my injury was an ASIA B. My spinal cord was being severely compressed, which was depriving my entire lower half of nutrition and blood supply. Quick anatomy lesson here: Your spinal cord has a thin sheath around it called the dura. This is what keeps your spinal fluid in. In my situation, the dislocated vertebrae were pressing into my dura. Not to mention I had two shattered vertebrae rubbing against it. Imagine a pin pushing on a balloon but not popping it. If any of those bone fragments broke through, the dura would have been ruptured, and I would have leaked out my spinal fluid. Game over. So Matt needed to decompress my cord, remove the bone fragments, realign my spine, and fuse it back together with screws and rods.

It was 7:25 when I was wheeled up to the operating room. That's less than an hour from the moment of impact on Providence Road. I was intubated and put on the operating table. That's the first time Matt got to see me. Not my best angle—out cold and facedown. He immediately did a maneuver where he grabbed me under the armpits and had someone else grab my pelvis, and they pulled in opposite directions. It's a technique used to try to realign a dislocation and un-pinch the spinal cord before an incision is ever made. It's not something all neurosurgeons try, but Matt did. And it worked. Matt bought me another forty-five minutes' worth of blood supply to my lower half.

Matt wasn't even really thinking at that point. He was on autopilot, just doing what he loved to do. He prepped me, made the incisions, put screws into the bone above the area that was dislocated, put screws in the level below, ran the rods through my spine, took all of the bone and ligament that was injured off my spinal cord, made sure there was no more pressure on it, then closed me up. It only took him an hour and ten minutes.

Then Matt left the OR to speak with my friends and family. Now, there is something about trauma surgeons you've probably heard before—about them not getting emotionally attached to patients. There needs to be a healthy professional boundary to be able to serve those who need them effectively. Matt's philosophy is no different. He always shows compassion. He prides himself on being positive, never giving false hope, and treating every single person from every walk of life equally. But he also keeps that emotional distance to protect himself and his patients.

Something happened to Matt, however, the moment he came into that small room. He expected to see one, maybe two people at the most. After all, it was only a seven-by-seven-foot room. Instead, he found like eight people all packed in there, Beth among them. And as he looked around the room at all those people—my loved ones who had taken their Saturday morning to offer support and hope together—he suddenly saw himself. That could have been *him* in surgery. That could have easily been his wife, his parents, his friends, crammed into that little room. Matt steadied himself and remained professional, but Beth saw the emotion come through.

He told them the extent of my injuries. "It's bad. But I'm really good at what I do. There's been no blood supply from the moment he was hit. But time is in our favor. If this had happened while he had been mountain biking, and let's say he was two hours from a hospital, this would have been a whole different story. So now that the blood supply is restored, his nerves will try to start firing again. We won't know the full extent of the damage for the next twenty-four or forty-eight hours, while he's recovering in the ICU." Then he looked at Beth directly. "We're watching for one thing. All I need to see is Dean move one of his toes. That's it. If he moves one toe, we have a chance, because that's the last nerve on the chain of the spinal cord."

Everyone had the same question: "So what are his chances of walking again?"

Matt told them straight. "With ASIA A patients, there's a 0 percent chance of ever walking again. With ASIA B patients like Dean, there's about a 2 percent chance."

The whole room replied, almost in unison: "You don't know Dean."

CHAPTER FIVE:

THE BATTLE BEGINS

When I was a kid, my dad took me on a bicycle ride in Finlay, Ohio. It was a race called the Horizontal Hundred, which is about as exciting as it sounds—one hundred miles through the cornfields of Ohio. In August. The epitome of super flat and super hot. Not long before that, we had done another race together in Brown County, Indiana, called the Hilly Hundred, and had a lot of fun. I thought this one would be just as cool.

We got about seventy-five to eighty miles into it and ended up taking a break beneath this big shade tree to get some water. By that point I was done. It was hot as hell, and I'd been pedaling all day. I was beyond tired. While I was busy resting and talking with another rider who was taking a break, my dad saddled back up and took off. When he realized I wasn't right behind him, he turned back around and peddled up the road.

He stopped where I was just sitting and hanging out. "Son, get your ass on that bicycle right now. We're not done yet. You're gonna finish the ride."

And I did.

Screw trying. I intended to finish the ride.

That memory, that lesson, and those words—finish the ride—come back to me from time to time. Like when I woke up post-op. Beth was there. She told me what Matt had said about my injuries. She told me what he said about me trying to move my toe. Screw trying. I intended to finish the ride.

Matt McGirt came to check on me early that next morning in the ICU. It was about twenty-four hours after I was hit by a truck while riding my bike. It was also the first time either of us got to look the other in the eyes.

I was awake and smiling. It wasn't just the pain meds. I've always been an early riser to Beth's eternal dismay. She was just coming to life in one of those super-uncomfortable chairs they put in the room for loved ones to sleep in.

"Hey, are you the doctor who fixed me?" I asked.

Matt nodded, a little taken aback. He was probably wondering if he was even in the right room. Later, he told me most people with ASIA B injuries are understandably depressed right after surgery. Oftentimes, they've spent all night paralyzed, looking at the ceiling, angry, sad. Not me. I spent all night focusing on my toe.

"Get over here," I said. "Look. I stayed up all night working on this."

It might have just been a few millimeters, but I wiggled my big toe. Beth started to cry. Matt grinned. He was hopeful, but statistically speaking I had 98 percent of the odds stacked against me. Even given Matt's wildly successful career as a top-rated neurosurgeon, he'd never had a patient beat ASIA B. Nor did he have one act the way I was acting on day one of paralysis. But he wasn't going to burst my bubble. Or maybe I just put the trauma surgeon in a state of shock.

"You stayed up all night working on your toe?" he asked.

I nodded. "Are you a runner?"

"Well, I was a sprinter at Duke. I never ran more than a few miles."

"I just ran a half marathon over in London six days ago," I told him. "And I'm going to run again. Why don't you and I raise some money for spinal cord patients and run a half marathon together. One year from now, to celebrate my recovery."

Matt was probably thinking there was no way in hell that was going to happen. "Sure. If you can pull it off, I'd be glad to join you."

Matt had been an outlier his whole life. He'd been an overachiever, a scrapper. So maybe he recognized some of those qualities in me. But he probably wondered what made me different from all his other patients in similar circumstances. He probably wondered what gave me the extra drive and determination to move that toe. What gave me the strength to fight when the odds were overwhelmingly against me? What made me want to finish the ride?

Matt didn't know why or how. But Beth did. She knew I'd been here before. Not in the same way with the same sort of injuries. The scars I carried inside were from another kind of pain. The kind that comes from humiliation. From shame. From rising and falling and getting back up again to battle the demons of addiction.

My journey to walking again actually started decades earlier. In middle school I was pretty restless. I got into trouble at school a lot. I wasn't smoking pot or drinking a lot. Yet. I wasn't even cutting school or getting in fights. But I was disruptive. I wanted to draw attention to myself. I did that by constantly talking in class—cracking jokes, making fun of people, making fun of my teachers. I spent a ton of time in the hall because my teachers would get fed up with me disrupting their class. I get it now. I didn't get it then though. I played the victim card to my parents. It wasn't my fault. The teachers were jackasses. When my parents would get called into school for conferences with my teachers, I would tell them I would try harder. That was usually a lie. The cycle would repeat. End of the day, I wasn't getting the education my parents thought I needed to succeed, so off to private school I went.

For eighth grade, I was accepted to Kentucky Country Day School (KCD). They had just built a new campus, and it wasn't exactly out in the country as the name implied. The school had been around for several decades in a suburban Louisville location, adjacent to Seneca Park and the Rock Creek Equestrian Center. But Louisville was growing and so was the school, so they had to expand.

Middle school is pretty damn awkward as it is. The KCD model was to move the eighth graders in with the high school classes. So instead of nine through twelve, KCD was eight through twelve. Imagine having these newly minted teenagers walking the same halls with kids who could drive, kids who were smoking and drinking and having sex. Pretty damn awkward became pretty damn cool! We were like high schoolers in eighth grade.

To make the transition easier, the school had a Big Brother/Big Sister program that connected seniors with eighth graders to mentor them. In theory, it's a great idea. In practice, maybe not so much. Some kids got hooked up with a cool senior and ended up having someone who would take them to parties and let them smoke or drink or both. I got a very square, straight-laced gal who I only remember meeting once, then she was back to focusing on her schoolwork.

But being tossed into a school where I didn't know many people really sucked. I knew a couple of kids that I went to grade school with, who made the move to private school at an earlier grade—Danny Tafel and Matt O'Brien. They were good kids who I had known since third and fifth grade, respectively. But the others I didn't know. And many of them came from backgrounds of privilege. They lived in bigger houses. Their parents drove nicer cars. They belonged to nicer clubs. They went on fancy vacations all the time.

The whole deal made me feel pretty less-than. I made some friends there. Many of them I still call friends to this day. But in the moment I didn't feel a part of anything. I wanted to belong, and I didn't. Most of these kids had gone to private schools their whole lives. Plus, the school's academics were a lot more rigorous than I was used to in public school. In the years before, I could hang just fine. But suddenly I had to work at it.

When eighth grade wrapped, I did well enough to get invited back. But I begged my parents to let me go to public school where I fit in. My power of persuasion worked. After some debate, I finally got what I wanted.

Back in the mid-1970s, Louisville, like several other southern cities, was transitioning to desegregated schools, then called "forced busing." So for one year or two, depending on one's last name, kids were bussed from their suburban home schools to a school in Louisville proper that served predominantly Black students. Put simply, the white kids went to the "Hood" for one year or two while the Black kids got bussed out to the 'burbs.

At first, it seemed like it was going to be a disaster all around. We were just emerging from an energy crisis nationally—and had a serious smog-pollution problem locally in Louisville—so people were really upset with spending so much money on busses and fuel, or so they said. At schools during the first fall there were fights and small riots breaking out on all sides, and we even had National Guardsman riding busses and patrolling schools to help keep the peace.

My older sister, Stacy, was bussed to Central High School her freshman year instead of going to the private girls' school our parents wanted her to attend. If you're a boxing fan, you may know Central because both Muhammad Ali and Olympian Greg Page graduated from there. In fact, Greg Page went to the Olympics when he was a senior and Stacy was a freshman. For whatever reason, she loved it. In fact, she loved it so much that she volunteered to stay her next three years and graduated from there. I knew if she loved it, I certainly was going to hate it.

But a pretty wonderful thing happened. Central had kids from all over the county with all sorts of different ethnic and socio-economic backgrounds. We had preppies, geeks, brothers, and freaks. Rednecks, potheads, drunks, and druggies. Jocks and band campers, musicians and artists, all mixed together in this wonderful "inner-city" school with no air conditioning and sparse resources when compared to Louisville's suburban high schools.

But it was a beautiful thing. I loved it! I made friends fast and really felt a part of everything. I got rid of my glasses and got contacts. Suddenly, I went from an awkward kid in a small pond, who never quite felt like I measured up, to a popular kid in a school full of people from everywhere where I totally fit in.

I made the freshman basketball team, the swim team, and the track team. I wasn't outstanding at any of them, but I was good enough. I had tons of friends, and girls suddenly took an interest in me. Over the following summer, one of my swimming teammates, Tom Willingham, talked me into trying out for the cross-country team. I had always thought of myself as more of a sprinter than an endurance runner. But what the heck—it was another team and a season in which I needed a sport. So I joined, and we started training together in the hot, humid, smoggy Ohio River Valley summer.

Tom and his brother Ben were literally in the cool club—a high school fraternity called the Athenaeum Literary Association (ALA). It's actually the oldest club of its kind in the country, a high school fraternity founded in 1892. But as highbrow as it sounds, this apparent bastion of literary excellence is just a cover for a drinking club for underage boys. They even had a sister organization, Dasmine, that was pretty much the same thing for girls. Louisville has long been home to the oldest high school fraternity and sorority system in the US. And Louisville is a hard-drinking town.

My longtime friends, Jim Frentz and Bill Brymer, were also members. They invited me to one of their parties where I met everyone else. Even some of the cool kids from KCD were in ALA. Suddenly, the tables had turned, and I no longer felt like an outcast. Everyone was cool and nice. Hot girls were giving me the time of day. I knew if I could join that fraternity, I'd really be living the dream.

But Mom and Dad said no. I was devastated. I remember thinking, *How could my parents do this to me?* Being denied such an opportunity didn't last long. I turned up the charm and turned down the obnoxiousness. I buckled down in school, stayed out of trouble, and didn't fight with my sister. In the end, I wore my parents down, and they let me join.

As nice as my ALA brothers were to me during rush, they were far less accommodating to me for the three weeks of pledging. The first night is paradoxically called Opening Morning. So we partied up until midnight, then the other pledges and I were driven to Ogden's Field for the opening festivities. Which sucked. Big-time. They threw all this nasty crap on us that they called "concoctions"—pretty much anything that smelled bad and made you want to vomit. Which many of us did.

We did a lot of running. We had to memorize history about the club and recite it on demand. If we got an answer wrong, more crap was thrown on us. Then there were the flour balls—eggs that had been cracked on our heads, then mixed with cold beer and flour, then put on our private parts. And for a little extra torture, a few squirts of tabasco sauce turned up the heat. Not a fun evening.

As miserable as that experience was, we bonded together and made it through the next three weeks of pledging, hazing, shoe shining, history reciting, car washing, cigarette buying, and bartending. I was an ALA member and I had finally arrived. At least in my own mind.

I had transformed into this super preppy, hardcore jock—Izod with the flipped collar, patch madras shorts—the whole nine yards. I was smoking cigarettes. And drinking even more. Cutting school. But I also met one of my best friends in the entire world during those ALA years—David Schneider. He probably lived three miles from me growing up. His parents had been going through a divorce when I befriended him. I helped him through that, which really solidified our friendship. We were always together. Well, either me and David or me and Paul Parker, another lifelong buddy who grew up five houses down from me on Starmont Road and I talked into joining ALA.

By the time senior year came around, I had moved back to my home school, Ballard High School, so I didn't play any sports. My grades were okay. Good enough to get by. Good enough to get into Kentucky. At the time, fogging up a mirror that was stuck under your nose would have qualified you. David ended up going to Hampden-Sydney, where he played football. I didn't get to see him much, except when we were back home for Christmas and other holidays. But we stayed in touch and remained good friends.

It was during my time at Kentucky that my excessive drinking first started catching up with me. My first semester I did pretty well.

That is, I kept my grades up enough to get into Delta Tau Delta. It's amazing what you can accomplish when you have the motivation to apply yourself. But beyond that, college was one long string of parties interrupted by classes. I majored in marketing. Not because I loved it, but because it had the easiest classes I could pass on a buzz. I even tried to pass a test on acid once. The results were not good.

My grades were suffering. So were my parents. They were getting sick of footing the bill for my paid vacation. So in December of 1987, I dropped out and moved back home with Mom and Dad. Which really wasn't home anymore, because they had sold our house on Starmont Road in Louisville and moved to Dublin, Ohio. Muirfield Village. The place Jack Nicklaus built.

I held a lot of resentment for that move. I mean, Kentucky had been my whole life. It was part of my identity. I'd grown up in that house. But I tried to move on. I got my Series 7 license and landed a job in Columbus selling mutual funds and insurance. I hated it. I hated the cold calling. I hated the cold weather. Not a ton of luck with the girls in Columbus either!

So when David called me from Atlanta and said he and a buddy from college were looking for another roommate, I was all in. A fresh start in a new city was just what I needed ... or what I thought I needed anyway.

A fresh start in a new city was just what I needed ... or what I thought I needed anyway.

Because in the back of my mind, I always thought a fresh start meant that maybe the drinking part would go away.

CHAPTER SIX:

THE FALLING

I don't think most people really grasp what an alcoholic looks like. At twenty-two years old, I sure didn't. You picture somebody out of work, living under a bridge, sipping on something sticking out of a paper bag. The funny thing is: most alcoholics are super-high functioning. At least before it gets really bad. They're your neighbors, your friends, your family members. They drink more than the recommended limit on more than one occasion. They may have their "go-to" drinks, but they are not necessarily discerning about what goes into their bodies.

I would drink wine, beer, liquor—whatever was around. And once I started, I wouldn't stop like everyone else did. Thankfully, I was never a mean drunk, like many. I wouldn't get really obnoxious. I might have been a little loud. I have a booming voice. But I'd just drink and be happy until I literally passed out. Which is probably why it went on for so long.

> **You can change zip codes all you want, but until *you* change, nothing is going to change.**

You can change zip codes all you want, but until *you* change, nothing is going to change. Such was the case with the move to Atlanta. I packed up my Honda Prelude, and off I went to live with David. I continued to drink and party. And I managed to get a job selling office supplies, which paid for my drinking and partying but not much else. That's when my dad gave me another one of those life-changing talks. He said, "Dean, do you want to be a participant in life, or do you want to be a spectator?"

Leave it to Dad to give me the kick in the rear I needed. That was the start of me getting back on track in life. Not necessarily with my drinking problem, but at least with my motivation problem. Suddenly, I wanted to get back into school. Not just to get by anymore, but to do *well*. I couldn't enroll in Georgia State because my grades from Kentucky were so bad, so I put in a couple of semesters at the DeKalb Community College and got my grades up. Once I got to Georgia State, I did great. Because I went to class. I studied for the tests. And I applied myself. In fact, I made the dean's list for my entire time at Georgia State and graduated with a BBA.

It was while I was in school in Atlanta that I met Beth while working at The Public House—a high-end restaurant set within a beautiful, old, antebellum building that was backed up to the Chattahoochee River. It actually used to be a hospital during the Civil War. Lots of history there—I mean for the building *and* for me and Beth.

I was immediately smitten and couldn't wait for my parents to meet her. They eventually made the trip down to Atlanta and loved her just as much as I did. She was suddenly a part of the kind of family she had always dreamed of. And what was even cooler was the fact that David and Beth really adored each other. Probably because they both had a vested interest in me. My best friend got me to Atlanta where I met my soulmate. Without both of them in my life, I might not even be here right now.

The thing about people who love you is that they don't always tell you what you want to hear. They tell you what you *need* to hear. Which really sucks when you don't want to hear something. Like the first time Beth and David attempted an intervention for my drinking.

Beth and I had been dating for about six months when David had called her one afternoon. He'd come home early and found me putting down a bottle of wine by myself. David had known I was a heavy drinker. In high school, he was the one who'd bring me home when I was too shitfaced to drive. My mom absolutely loved David. She was always super strict, but there he would be, bringing me home drunk a half hour after my curfew. Somehow, because David was there, we'd always get away with it.

But now that we were legit adulting—with a good job and a serious relationship on the line—David started getting concerned. He told Beth he thought I had a problem with alcohol. Beth ended up talking about it to my mom, and my aunt, and my sister. So I agreed to go to a twelve-step program in Midtown. Interesting side note: while we were there, a well-known, internationally renowned celebrity stood up and acknowledged their struggle with addiction. True story. But even that wasn't inspiring enough for me to stick with it.

I went a couple of times and then, well, I just stopped. Because I really didn't think I needed it. And Beth and I started getting caught in a very unhealthy dynamic. Remember her childhood? She came from a past filled with feelings of rejection and abandonment. And when I was drunk, all my walls would come down, and I'd suddenly transform into a very sensitive, very affectionate person with Beth. A lot more attentive and affectionate than I usually am. Beth of course loved that attention. It probably filled a gap for her … in an unhealthy way. Not that she ever encouraged or condoned the extent of my drinking. It was absolutely the opposite in fact. But especially in those early years, I wasn't really hurting anyone but myself. And I was filling a void for her. So it continued.

Beth and I dated for three and a half years before we got married. Three years after that we had our first child, Will. Five and a half years after that, Grace came along. We both had good jobs—Beth was working in sales for a corrugated paper company, while I was in sales for Pillsbury. Life was humming along nicely in Buckhead, Atlanta. Except for my drinking. Which, if you've ever lived with a high-functioning alcoholic, is like a splinter in your foot that you try to ignore. You walk on it so much that eventually you get used to the pain. You know deep down it's an issue, but you just don't feel the necessity to get help. Sooner or later though, that splinter gets infected. It festers. Then it spreads to other parts of your body and causes systemic issues.

The years wore on for Beth and me, and the festering continued. We'd be out with friends, or having dinner at home, and I'd just drink until I was out cold. Beth would shake me, bump me, tap me. Nothing. There I'd sit with my head bowed. And Beth would be left to make excuses. Part of the cycle was for me to wake up the next morning with my tail between my legs, feeling guilty and ashamed. Then I'd make breakfast for Beth and the kids as a way of saying, "I'm sorry." Which really did nothing but reinforce Beth's emotional needs and pacify my guilt until the next time. And the next time.

Once when I worked for Womble Carlyle, I was out with some of my coworkers for a huge black tie event. I'd gotten so drunk—and my colleagues were so afraid of what Beth might do—that they rang the doorbell at 1:00 a.m., threw me in the bushes by the door, then ran off. Another time, we were renovating our home and I couldn't find a bottle opener. So I somehow thought it was a good idea to use the sharpened end of a broomstick that I'd whittled to a point for use in our outdoor firepit. Sharp objects and drunks don't exactly mix well. I'm lucky I didn't put my eye out. But I did manage to scratch my cornea and give myself a huge shiner.

Unfortunately, that wasn't my only close call. One night it was super late, and I'd been out entertaining clients. Beth and the kids were all asleep. So I crept upstairs and tapped Beth on the shoulder and told her she needed to come downstairs right away. Beth and I went down to meet the police officer standing in our kitchen, who had just pulled me over for driving while intoxicated. He handed Beth my car keys and told her our car was in a parking lot on Randolph Road, and that I was damn lucky he was too exhausted to take me all the way downtown to process me for a DUI.

Having come out on the other side of all of this, I've forgiven myself for a lot of things.

Having come out on the other side of all of this, I've forgiven myself for a lot of things. But I still have a lot of regret. One of the biggest regrets is about David. While he was dying, I was busy drinking.

I can't remember exactly when he got sick, but it was right around the time Beth and I moved to Charlotte. He was in Louisville and had only recently met the love of his life, Cathy—an amazing woman and dear friend. David was one of those super athletes who was in great shape and doing triathlons all the time. Unlike me. He was actually training for a triathlon when he started feeling really low on energy. Melanoma, the specialists determined. They put him on a cocktail of chemo they called "the kitchen sink treatment." It was working, but it was also killing him.

David was a fighter though. If he hadn't been in such fantastic physical shape, he never would have lasted eleven more years. He went on about his life and ended up having two amazing boys with Cathy. The cancer continued to eat him alive. He had to have so many surgeries—parts of his lungs, brain, spleen, and liver were removed.

It was Mother's Day, twelve years ago as of this writing, when Beth and I went to see him for what ended up being the last time. By then David's voice was really high and raspy. He'd lost so much weight that, when I hugged him, I felt like I was hugging a skeleton.

David had always been a dog lover and had three beautiful labs at the time. We had just gotten a labradoodle named Blue and brought her along. When David and I were roommates, there were two creeks that came together in our backyard in Buckhead, with an island where the confluence was. On the day we visited, it was just packed with his dogs. All labs, all beautiful, just playing and jumping and running. Sitting there, watching those dogs with David, a huge grin on his face, is one of those memories that will live in my heart and mind until the day I die. He was gone two weeks later.

I felt sick with guilt afterward. Maybe if I hadn't been drinking so heavily, I would have had more time to spend with David. Maybe I should have gone to see him more. I ended up apologizing to Cathy at one point, but she wouldn't hear of it. "Dean, are you crazy? You did the best you could, when you could. Every time you were in town, you always called and came over. David loved you. And he knew you loved him."

I like to think that David knows what's in my heart now. That he's an angel, always looking out for me, just like he used to. Like when

Beth decided it was time for a final intervention. I'd reached the end of my self-destructive behavior and denial.

I now had to choose between my family and my addiction.

CHAPTER SEVEN:
THE RISING

The intervention that Beth set in motion definitely wasn't easy on me. But it was hell on Beth. After all, I could have told her and everybody else to kiss my ass. I could have packed up and walked away from my family. Thank God I had the strength and courage not to do those things. But prior to the intervention, Beth really didn't know *how* I'd react. She hoped. She had faith. But that's very different than knowing for sure.

The thing is: choosing alcohol over my family was only part of Beth's fear. Before the day arrived, she told my mom and sister that it was the hardest decision she had ever had to make in her life. Coming from a childhood of rejection creates an unhealthy dynamic. When I was drunk, I was super affectionate and open. Not that sober me isn't loving and empathetic. It's just that being under the influence dropped my walls a bit more, which is exactly what Beth craved. So her fear was: *Would sober Dean mean that I suddenly lose all that closeness that I've come to expect?*

In the end, she loved me enough to want what was best for *me*, not herself. Which tells you exactly how blessed I am to be her husband. If you're ever searching for an example of the word *love*, that's it—unselfish sacrifice.

Alcoholism is very much like the proverbial house of cards.

The events leading up to the day were probably pretty typical as far as interventions go. A culmination of years of ignoring the white elephant in the room, then, all of a sudden, one binge too many. Alcoholism is very much like the proverbial house of cards. You build it as high as you can, adding as many cards as you can, until that last card sends everything toppling to the ground. A place known as Rock Bottom. That place, and the journey to find Rock Bottom, is different and more or less extreme for every alcoholic. In the grand scheme of things, my elevator didn't go all the way down to bedrock. My elevator ended up in a pretty nice bargain basement. I hadn't lost anything … yet. I still had my house, my job, all my material possessions. I had never had a DUI and had never been arrested. But I was about to lose the one thing that was my most valued possession … my family.

My final card came during one of our family fun nights, just Beth and me and our kids. We had all gone out to eat, then came home to the backyard where we toasted some marshmallows.

True to form, I had way too much to drink. And one of the things I liked to do when I was drunk was play music. Loud music. Very loud music. It annoyed the hell out of Beth.

She asked me to turn it down, so I went inside and headed over to the stereo receiver to adjust the volume. I knelt in front of it, then got distracted looking for a song I wanted to play. That's the last thing I remember. When I didn't return, Beth came into the house to look for me, with my seven-year-old daughter, Grace, in tow. They found me sitting there, crossed-legged, chin on my chest, passed out. Beth couldn't wake me up. My little girl was frightened.

That's the moment Beth knew this routine couldn't go on much longer without it causing harm to our kids or to myself. So she gave me an ultimatum: get help, or else things were going to change between us. I love my wife and family, so I was prepared to do anything for them. I went to the best of the best in Charlotte—renowned psychotherapist Kim Honeycutt.

I saw Kim for about three months. But the thing about addiction is that recovery starts from the inside. And inside, I wasn't ready. To me, drinking wasn't a problem. So what if I fell asleep? I never hurt anyone. I wasn't a mean drunk. Hell, excessive drinking was part of the culture I'd grown up in. It was part of who I was. Drinking wasn't just condoned at an early age; it was encouraged.

What I didn't understand was that alcoholism affects brain function. It creates a nasty feedback loop by hijacking the pleasure/reward system in the brain. Long-term alcohol abuse also damages the prefrontal cortex, the part of the brain that's used for rationality and decision-making. I may have had my own reasons, but like it or not, I was dependent on alcohol—not just emotionally, but chemically. That wasn't going to change until I got the kind of help rehabilitation provides.

After my final session with Kim, I came home and told Beth that she had said I was all good. Beth thankfully knew better. She called Kim and got the real story: Kim told me she had helped me all she could. If I wanted to get sober, I had to take the next step. Clearly, I wasn't prepared to do that on my own.

Beth, however, didn't give up.

She called my sister, my aunt, her parents, my parents, her brothers—everyone who loved me and wanted me to get help. Those who couldn't come wrote letters. Beth coordinated everyone to be in town the day of the intervention, and she asked Kim to facilitate. So I went out for my morning run and returned to a bunch of cars parked in the circular driveway in front of my house.

Deep down I knew the gig was up. I knew what was happening. I went around to come in the back gate, and there was Kim.

"What's up?" she said.

"What's up with you?"

"My friend," Kim said, "I'm here to do an intervention."

It's difficult to describe what I felt at that moment. I know what I *didn't* feel. I didn't feel bitter or resentful. I didn't feel angry or hurt or offended. I suppose I felt some shame and embarrassment. But most of all, if I had to sum up how I felt in one word, it would be: *relieved.*

Kim and I went inside. There was Beth and all my loved ones sitting in a circle. And an empty chair. I filled that chair, and I listened to my loved ones share with me how my alcoholism affected their lives. How much they cared about me, and how they wanted me to be sober and healthy so I could make new memories with each of them.

I was calm through the whole intervention. I soaked it all in. And when everyone was done, I went around the house with Kim and got rid of all the weed and booze. Then Kim looked at me and said, "Now you have two choices: you can either go to outpatient rehab, or you can leave."

I was ready. I opted for door number one, outpatient rehab, which lasted for twelve weeks. I met some amazing people there, people who are as close to me now as family. But more importantly, I got sober, and have stayed that way for twelve years at the time of this writing.

Beth says she has always admired my willpower. When I set my mind to doing something, I don't stop until it happens. Years earlier, when I had made up my mind to give up cigarettes, that was it. The last one I had was really the last one I ever had.

It was that kind of drive and willpower that led me to running at a high level in my first few years of sobriety. I started off slow but eventually built up my endurance and strength to where I could reach the goals I set for myself. First a half marathon. Then a marathon. Then more half marathons. Then working and training to hit a particular time goal. Then crushing that goal! It was in doing the things that were difficult—the things others gave up on—that I found out who Dean Otto really was.

I had to find a higher power and turn my will and my life over to that.

My recovery from addiction took more than just willpower. I needed more than that. I needed a spiritual solution, and I was spiritually bankrupt. I found that solution in a twelve-step recovery program. I had to surrender to win at this fight. This was not something I was programmed for, but I was willing. I had to find a higher power and turn my will and my life over to that.

Next, I cleaned house by making a list of those I had harmed and those I held resentments against and shared that list with another man. I asked God to remove my character defects, those that stood in the way of me helping others. Next, I made amends to those I had harmed. And finally, I had to do the most rewarding part of my recovery journey. I had to give it all away! I had to help the next guy do what I had just done. And that's how we roll! That's the dessert. *Nothing* gives me a better feeling than helping others.

Setting goals and reaching them was who I was. Goals like staying sober one day at a time. Goals like fighting through the pain and exhaustion as I raced toward the finish line to make the time I had set for myself.

Goals like wiggling my toe when the doctor said I had a 2 percent chance of ever walking again.

As miraculous and monumental as that was, I was still frustrated I couldn't do more. A couple days went by in the ICU. Family and friends came in to visit. Then on the third day, after I had been moved to the main hospital, the nurses came into my room to try to get me out of bed so I could walk to the bathroom. If you've ever had the misfortune of being in a hospital, you know the rooms aren't very big. The distance from my bed to the bathroom was probably less than five feet. A couple steps.

They placed a walker near the edge of my bed and helped me sit up. Using every ounce of strength I had, I pulled myself up until I was standing. My legs were shaking uncontrollably. The pain was excruciating as I willed myself to take a step. Then I took another. I focused on my goal—the bathroom. It wasn't a glamorous goal, but to me it might as well have been the summit of Mount Everest. And I made it!

I wasn't graceful. I wasn't fast. But three days after I'd been hit by a truck that shattered my spine I was rising.

CHAPTER EIGHT:

THE PURPOSE

Dean. Charlotte, North Carolina. Bike accident.

Those were the only buzzwords Will Huffman had at his disposal about me. For days he kept coming up empty on Facebook, on Google, even searching police reports. And then, less than a week after he accidently hit me with his truck, he had a breakthrough. My trainer, Kelly, posted a picture of me. Will recognized my face right off.

By scrolling through the comments, Will found my last name. Then he found Beth's Facebook page. Will asked his wife, Jeanelle, to reach out to Beth. So Jeanelle sent a message saying they didn't want to overstep any boundaries of privacy but wanted Beth and me to know they were praying for us. She also asked if we could share any details about my condition.

Beth responded and gave some insight into where things stood with my health. Understandably, Will was taken aback by the extent of my injuries. You have to remember, when he left the scene, it's not like there was blood everywhere. I had some road rash. But I was lucid and talking. The police were concerned, obviously, but not overly so.

Will gave Beth his phone number. The next Saturday morning, exactly one week from the date of the accident, Beth called Will and Jeanelle. She ended up speaking to Jeanelle first for about thirty to forty-five minutes. Then she spoke with Will for another forty-five minutes. Beth filled them both in about my miraculous recovery.

By that time I had been moved to a regular hospital room. I had gone from shuffling to the bathroom that first day out of bed, to shuffling to the door the next day, to shuffling fifty feet down the hallway with my walker on the following day. By the fourth day, they happily kicked me out of the main hospital and next door to inpatient rehab.

Dr. McGirt was stunned. Beth was in tears. I was excited. I was grateful. But I was also like, "Um, yeah. I told you so. We have a half marathon to run this time next year. What's next?"

Will had been out of town for work when he and Beth connected. But as soon as he got back that following Monday, he and Jeanelle came for a visit. He was already familiar with the hospital, as the company he worked for, Otis, did the elevator maintenance. They walked to the elevator doors. Will pushed out a breath and pressed the button. He was anxious and glad to have his wife by his side.

The young couple had been married less than a year at that point. The accident was the first major event they had to weather together— hopefully one of the last ones too. It all happened so fast that Will had a hard time processing everything. Like Beth was for me, Jeanelle was Will's rock. She listened. She was supportive. She tried to be that voice of reason in Will's storm of worry.

Worry can actually be a blessing and a curse. It can be all-consuming. But it also causes you to be cautious. Thankfully, Will is a self-proclaimed worrier. For a twenty-seven-year-old, he was not only insured but very well insured. Just in case a tree fell on his house. Just in case his dog bit the mailman. Just in case he was driving one Saturday morning to a football game at his alma mater and accidently hit a bicyclist.

The truth of it is: no matter how things would have turned out, I had zero intent to ever sue Will Huffman. Even if he didn't have the insurance that provided for my surgery, hospital care, and rehabilitation. I believe he knew that from the moment I forgave him when I was laying there broken on Providence Road. At least I hope he did.

But accidents are just that ... *accidents.*

He had friends warn him about speaking with me, admitting to anything, discussing the accident. But accidents are just that ... *accidents.* They happen, and it's our character that determines how we deal with them.

I like to think that Will came to see me with a heart free and clear of fear. When he and Jeanelle came in the room, I was laying in bed, in good spirits. Jeanelle sat with Beth at the foot of the bed. Will took a seat next to me. We talked for probably two hours—very little of it about the accident. We talked about our faith and our families. I learned Will's mother was named Beth. And he learned I had a son named Will. We talked about the future, about what we were going to do to make something good come out of our paths crossing in the way they did. I just wasn't quite sure what that was yet.

When I was transferred to the rehabilitation unit, my friend and the guy who fixed all my aches and pains from running, Dr. Scott Greenapple, showed up. He had been my chiropractor and acupuncturist for years, manipulating me, sticking needles in me, and stretching me whenever I was sore or banged up from running. Scott is a legend around Charlotte and worked on many of the professional and amateur athletes in town. Very skilled at his craft and an all-around great guy. Because we're Facebook friends, he had read about the accident and came right away to see me.

He brought his camera because he couldn't believe his eyes. He said something to the effect of: "Dude, you have no freaking idea what you're doing right now. I've never seen anything like this. I don't know how to explain it. You're one in a million, man. *Nobody* does this."

"I made up my mind that I'm walking out of this place," I said. "And that's exactly what I'm going to do."

Scott was there, spotting me and cheering me on when I took my first two steps up this little platform they make you get on and off. Every single day I was making more and more progress. I'd work out three times a day, come back to the bed and collapse. I'd take a pain pill. I'd go to sleep. Then I'd wake up and do it all again.

I hadn't yet been there a week when I saw a teenage kid in a wheelchair, sitting there looking despondent, his mother next to him. I was making my way around the perimeter of the rehab facility, hanging onto things as I went. The mom struck up a conversation with me as I passed.

"What happened?"

"I got hit by a truck."

She put her hand to her mouth. "Wow. While walking?"

"No, I was riding my bike. It shattered my spine."

"My goodness. How long ago was that?"

"Oh, about a week ago."

I thought her jaw was going to hit the floor. She sat forward. "What? You're doing this after a week?"

"Yeah, I couldn't feel anything. I was paralyzed from the waist down. But I've made this crazy recovery, and now I'm just like, trying to get back everything I can as fast as I can."

Her son was sitting there, listening. She told me he'd been in a car accident.

I turned to him. "Hey, how old are you?"

"Eighteen."

"Well, I'm fifty-one. And if my old ass can get out of a wheelchair and walk around this room, then you can too."

I left and didn't really think any more about it. I finished my walk. I took a nap. I came back for my afternoon workout.

At that moment I understood why God had chosen me.

And as soon as I walked in, that kid was on a walker, taking his first steps. I fought back tears as I watched him. At that moment I understood why God had chosen me.

I had discovered my purpose. And three weeks later, I walked on my own two feet out of that place.

CHAPTER NINE:

THE COMEBACK

Graham Claytor knew I was going to be a special case when I hobbled into his physical therapy clinic at the right time on the wrong day. Freshly discharged from my inpatient therapy, I was barely getting around on a walker. But at least I was getting around. Now, my goal was to get my mobility back to where it was before the accident. I didn't just plan on walking again. I wanted to run. I wanted to race. I wanted to cross the finish line again.

That meant a lot of pain. A lot of hard work. A lot of frustration. A lot of coaching. According to Dr. McGirt, if anyone could get me back to running, it was Graham. He'd built his clinic from the ground up and led a team of highly skilled physical therapists for over eighteen years. Getting people like me to reach our goals is what he specialized in. Professional golfers and NASCAR drivers were among his patients—people who not just wanted to get their game back but *needed* to get their game back.

Matt McGirt had prepped Graham prior to my visit: Survivor of a tragic accident. Fracture to the lower thoracic and upper lumbar.

ASIA B. Not anticipated to walk again. Miraculously ambulatory within days of the accident.

I was ready to start my comeback. The clock was ticking.

Coming into his clinic on the wrong day was an honest mistake. I know I probably annoyed the hell out of the office staff, but I made it clear I wasn't turning back. Matt McGirt had basically given me an eighteen-month countdown. Whatever mobility I was able to get back, I'd get it back in that time. After eighteen months, it was over. So whatever my appointment day was supposed to be didn't matter. I was ready to start my comeback. The clock was ticking.

Part of what gives Graham a guidepost for the potential of his patients is their preoperative mentality. That for him is the biggest predictor of postoperative success. So before Beth and I even came into the clinic that first day, Graham knew that my mind was either going to be my greatest ally or my worst enemy.

Needless to say, my stubbornness gave Graham a pretty good indication of my mentality. I wobbled my ass back into one of the open rooms, sat myself down, and waited with Beth to be seen. Graham wasn't sure if he could even fit me in between other patients, but somehow he made it work. I'm eternally grateful he did.

Graham is a no-nonsense, no sugarcoating kind of guy. That's what I love about him the most. Well, that and he's a huge college basketball fan. His only downside is that Graham is a Carolina Tar Heels fan, while I root for the Kentucky Wildcats. Despite that difference, we hit it off right away. Within the first thirty seconds of our visit, I told him my goal of running a half marathon—13.1 miles—on the anniversary of my accident. He said it was doable but would likely take ten to twelve months for full mobility. After all, I wasn't just coming in there with random lower back pain from digging in my backyard. I survived a massive accident and had my spine rebuilt with metal rods.

"The half marathon is ten months away," I told him. "We better get started."

I'd love to write that the days and weeks that followed went smoothly—that I trained and worked out and stretched and improved each and every day, with "Eye of the Tiger" from the film *Rocky* ringing out through the clinic. My progress was a lot more like the stock market. Incremental gains. Sometimes a few setbacks. Big leaps forward. Plateauing. The plateaus were the worst. I'd make it so far, then suddenly I couldn't bend and touch my toes, or twist left, or step up any faster. Or move the way I wanted to move. Sometimes my endurance was a lot lower than I hoped it would be.

Part of my challenge was my own physical limitation due to the fusion of my spine and the nerve damage. Nerves take a long time to heal. And fusion is a process that can take ten to twelve months for the vertebrae to stabilize and calcify together with all the screws and rods. If I pushed myself too hard, I could cause irreparable damage. So Graham had me on a pretty tight leash. One that I kept tugging at.

He had me on an exercise bike. He stretched me. He had me doing all sorts of exercises. It seemed like every day I asked him when he thought I'd be able to run again. He'd say, "Man, I'm just trying to get you walking out of this clinic on your own."

I kept pushing him, and myself. He'd give me exercises to do—I'd do them and say, "What's next?" He'd have me take medicine balls or weights and do abdominal exercises. Reaching exercises. Balance exercises. I slowly built my endurance up and got to the cardiovascular stage. Ten months to race day became nine months. Then eight months.

The pain was insane. I hurt the entire time. Hurt *bad*. Graham would have to treat me with pain-relieving modalities—massage, acupuncture, electrical stimulation. There were days I wanted to give up. There were days I was angry. But I knew deep down I could do it. I *knew* it. So I leaned on Beth, and my loved ones, and my faith. And Graham. He let me have my fits, left me alone when I got pissed off. Then he'd come back and ask if I was through and ready to get back to work.

Graham and I had that incredibly special coach-player relationship. He always steered my mind back to where I used to be. Where I wanted to be. And where I could have been.

"You're still here, dude. You're not dead. You're not paralyzed," he would say, and I would humbly push onward.

And so on I would go, grateful and hopeful. Living in the moment. It was a long and winding road, just like The Beatles sang about. But slowly, over time, I improved. I was walking. Then I was jogging. But Graham wouldn't let me run.

To say I was frustrated is an understatement. It had been four months since the accident. I felt great. Relatively speaking. Graham was just being a good coach, a good therapist. A good friend. He was doing exactly what he was supposed to do. But he didn't understand— I *needed* to start running. The date of the half marathon was creeping up.

Finally, he relented. "You can run one mile. That's it."

There are no words to describe how good that first mile felt. It was exhilarating. I felt myself coming alive again. As soon as I got back to the clinic: "Okay, can I run two miles now?"

"Sure," he said. "In two weeks."

So that's exactly what I did. But I also felt obligated to let him know about the Big Sur Marathon in April. If you've never heard of it, Big Sur is a race that's super hard to get into that basically works on a lottery-type system. I had signed up nearly a year earlier, way before the accident. And I signed up as a group with my buddies Tony, Zach, and Josh. That meant either all of us had to go, or none of us could go. I knew I couldn't run the whole thing. Or even half of it. But I needed to participate somehow.

"That's months away," he said. "We'll cross that bridge when we get to it."

In the meantime, I told Graham about a 5K coming up in a month that I wanted to sign up for. For those not great at math, that's 3.1 miles. He wasn't thrilled, but he agreed. My new favorite words in the English language quickly became "as tolerated."

By now it was late January 2017. Seven months to the half marathon and the one-year anniversary of my accident. I was running more, working myself up to the three-mile mark. One morning I was out training along at McAlpine Greenway. I've always enjoyed running, but the wind was blowing hard and had a chilly bite to it. The way it's set up with trees on both sides, it becomes sort of like a shoot when the wind picks up. Running into a hard, cold headwind was not what I wanted to do, so I ducked off onto the trail to Boyce Park near a small creek to finish my workout.

That move would prove to be divine. Of all the people in the world that I could run into, just a few yards away, there was Will Huffman with his wife Jeanelle, walking their dog.

They were just as shocked as I was. Just as glad as I was. We all gave each other big, sweaty hugs. Chatted briefly about what was going on in our lives. Will and I had never lost touch; we just didn't talk all the time.

"I just signed up for a 5K here in Charlotte, first week of March," I told them. "It's going to be my comeback race. I would love for you guys to run it with me."

Will was beaming. What I didn't know was that just days before, Jeanelle, for whatever reason, suggested that the couple take part in a 5K. So that morning, of all the places they could have been training, they picked the very same park, the very same path, the very same day.

"Dean, we would absolutely love to run with you. We'll be there," he said.

About a month later, Will and Jeanelle made good on their promise. It was an incredible race. My family and friends all painted signs and cheered me on. Michelle Boudin, a well-known broadcaster for our local NBC affiliate who had broken the story on my miraculous recovery months earlier, was there covering the race. It was an extremely emotional event for me. I can't explain it, but the gravity of what *could* have happened hit me. Hard. After the race, Will and Jeanelle wanted to go out to breakfast with me and my family. I just needed to be with those closest to me. Looking back, I regret that decision. Will and Jeanelle are great people and *are* like family. After that day, Will and I remained in touch much more often. And I had another race in mind for him—the half marathon Matt McGirt and I were planning on running in September.

By that time, the Big Sur Marathon was about a month away. I brought it up again during one of my physical therapy sessions at the clinic. Graham and Matt shot me down right away.

"Dean, it's not worth it. You could permanently damage yourself. Your spine isn't even fully fused yet," said Matt.

I gave it some thought. "How many miles can I run?"

"Four," he said.

What I heard was five or six. Then I turned on the charm. "All right, let's make a deal. What if I put a relay team together and I run five miles, then they split the rest of the race?"

A few weeks later, I was off to Big Sur, California. On the plane, Zach ended up talking to the guy sitting next to him—Joe Speed Demon. At least that's his handle on Facebook. Talk about an inspiration. At that point, Joe was seventy-five years old, with 350 marathons under his belt. And he was still running them in under four hours! He had on a Boston Marathon jacket, a race he had run just two weeks earlier. They actually have a thing called Big Sur to Boston—a back-to-back set of marathons within two weeks of each other. If you've never run a marathon, I can tell you firsthand that you feel you've been hit by a truck that first week after. Well, maybe not *exactly* like being hit by a truck. I should know. But your body is pretty beat up and worn out. Joe Speed Demon? This guy had done the Big Sur to Boston back-to-back *ten times!*

We arrived at Big Sur and hung out with Joe and other amazing athletes. The race itself was awesome. I ran the first leg for my relay team, as it was net downhill. Zach, Tony, and Josh each ran their own full marathon, but at least we got to run that first leg together, just like we had planned a year earlier.

Zach was probably the most competitive out of all of us, which is saying something because we're all pretty competitive. We had a pact to all run at least the first couple of miles together, then, well, just see what happened. Zach, however, was so wound up, at about three hundred yards he was like, "Gotta go, guys. Bye!"

He finished third behind Tony and Josh, which was hilarious. Tony ribbed him especially hard, called him "Bronze" for being third among the able-bodied in the group. Zach was not amused. Good times!

By then I was nine months out from my surgery. Matt and Graham checked and double-checked—the fusion in my spine was all good. Now it was a matter of slowly working my way up to my goal of the half marathon.

I needed to finish the ride. *The* ride.

I signed up for a 10K in Charlotte to see if I could pull it off. That one was tough. It ended up being three times hillier than I thought it was going to be. It was ninety degrees and miserable, but I finished it in an hour. Now I had to find out how I would do with ten miles. If I could do ten miles, I could do a half marathon. It went great.

Two things remained that I needed to do. I needed to finish the ride. *The* ride. The bike ride that led to the accident. And I needed to cross the finish line in the half marathon … with Will and Matt by my side—the man who gave me my life back and the man who gave me purpose.

CHAPTER TEN:
THE FINISH LINE

We're not done yet, Son. You're gonna finish the ride.

Dad's words became a mantra throughout my life to always finish what I start. I drive my kids and Beth nuts with them to this day. But those words had a special meaning, a prophetic ring to them in the months following the accident. I had driven Providence Road many times throughout my recovery. It was an eerie feeling. Like wandering back through a nightmare I'd awakened from. I had even been out there with Will and Matt for interviews and to take b-roll when producers from the *Today* show, *Ellen*, and other media outlets caught wind of the story.

But I never finished the ride—the ride that was unexpectedly interrupted when I was hit by a truck and nearly lost my ability to ever walk again. I knew deep down, at some point, that I *needed* to finish that ride. And I needed the effort to make an impact not just on me, but on others. That's how I ended up organizing my Finish the Ride fundraising event, benefitting the Adaptive Sports and Adventures Program (ASAP) for Atrium Health. They are an amazing organization that has been helping adults and children participate in adaptive sports for over two decades—people who have various physical challenges like amputation, brain injury, multiple sclerosis, and spinal cord injuries.

ASAP helps people participate in a variety of competitive and recreational adaptive sports including archery, swimming, hand-cycling, and tennis. So I thought, *What the heck? Why not finish my ride and raise a few thousand dollars for a great cause?*

So that's what we did. I coordinated the ride with a bunch of friends. I got a hold of a few of my fellowship buddies who were bikers—as in *motorcycles*, not bicycles—and asked them if they would ride their Harleys along with the twenty or so of us who were going to be biking, to protect us from traffic. They were all in.

The day of the ride was hotter than it had been in a while. I planned to take the exact same route the day I was hit, up Providence Road, then end up back at my house for a big barbecue. My biker buddies were like cops, stopping traffic at the intersections so we could all safely ride through. When we got to Providence, I had this bizarre feeling, like my body was remembering something that my mind wanted to forget. I could feel the *whoosh* of cars going by, which made the hackles on my neck stand up. To this day, when I'm just running or walking on a sidewalk, if I don't have my air pods in so I can totally tune everything else out, sometimes I get that feeling—like I need to brace for impact.

But the day of the Finish the Ride event couldn't have gone better. Will even joined the celebration back at the house after the ride. I'm glad he did for a couple of reasons: (1) we had over forty pounds of barbecue to eat, and (2) it was good for my cycling friends to meet the guy who hit me and realize that not all drivers are careless jerks. The thing about biking is that it's a very close-knit community—one that doesn't always think well of drivers. I get it—there are lots of obnoxious, rude, reckless motorists out there. But Will Huffman isn't one of them.

Will was understandably anxious, but he was readily accepted by the group. For the most part. And I was super proud of one of my friends who told Will that he admired his courage, that Will had changed his perspective of drivers and the accidents that do sometimes happen.

But the coolest part of the event was afterward, when I went back and Googled the date. It was within *two days* of the forty-year anniversary of that ride in Indiana with my dad. Seriously, you can't make this stuff up.

With that behind me, the last thing to check off my list was the Napa Valley Half Marathon with Matt and Will by my side, slated to take place on the one-year anniversary of the accident—September 24, 2017. The three of us wanted to make this run as big as we could, because we were going to raise as much money for ASAP as we could. Both *Ellen* and the *Today* show helped to make that possible. Originally, the producers of the shows were at arms, hoping to get an exclusive story. But I convinced them of a couple great angles that would appeal to each of their audiences: *Ellen* could be awesome daytime talk show TV—fun and engaging and emotional with the three of us on stage together. The *Today* show could do a more in-depth mini-documentary—interview us in Charlotte, then cover the race in Napa. The respective producers agreed.

About three weeks before the Napa Half, Matt, Will, and I all flew out separately to tape our segment for the first week of the new season of *Ellen*. Everybody involved in the show was an absolute class act. We got picked up and driven around in limos. We had our own dressing rooms, totally stocked with all kinds of food and drinks. It was an awesome experience.

The night we got into town, we all met up and had dinner in Hollywood. Then it was *on*. The next day we filmed from 7:30 a.m. until late afternoon. We spent the day taping separate interviews for the lead-in to the segment. The producers walked us through rehearsal of what would happen once we were on stage. We had a little downtime while we were waiting to go on, and someone said that Mark Wahlberg and Will Ferrell were on set filming another episode. To me, Will Ferrell is the funniest guy on the planet. I *needed* to see Will Ferrell. I mean, how could my all-time favorite actor be right in the same vicinity, and I don't at least try to meet him?

Matt and Will were nonbelievers. They both were like, "Dean, you're not going to meet Will Ferrell."

"The hell I'm not," I said, and snuck downstairs with my iPhone. Before long, there they were—Will Ferrell and Mark Wahlberg—playing a game of Pop-A-Shot that was being filmed for the show. So I whipped out my phone and filmed it too. It was awesome. Just as they finished, I felt a tap on my shoulder.

"Sir, you're going to have to delete that."

"I will," I said, and ran back upstairs. It's a little hard to remember because there was a lot going on that day, but I'm pretty sure I deleted the video. Like 98 percent sure.

We waited around in the Green Room a bit longer, and then just like you see on TV, we were told to head out on stage, around that big wall. I've never seen lights like that in my life—so incredibly bright, like staring into a thousand suns. They had prepped us on the questions to expect from Ellen, but they also said it's her show and she does whatever she wants, so she may ask us something totally different.

Ellen was a total pro, just as kind as could be. And we could tell she had really done her homework. She gave each of us a hug when we first got there and said something personal to each of us. It was so surreal being on stage with her. She pretty much stuck to the script the whole time. When we went to a commercial break, all these random people popped out of nowhere and touched up our makeup and refilled our waters. Ellen was really personable when we were off camera. Not to mention hilarious. Only she could get away with ribbing us that it was a little embarrassing that we were only running a half marathon in Napa instead of a full marathon.

When we came back from the break, Ellen did the unbelievable, as she often does. She presented me with a $20,000 check for ASAP. I had no clue such a generous gift was even coming. Just being on the show was thrilling enough. After we were through with our segment, she hugged each of us goodbye and said a little something again. To Will she said, "If I ever get hit by a truck, I hope you're driving it."

The next day, we hopped our flights home. Three weeks later, we were back at the airport and off to Napa. By then, word had spread far and wide about our story. Harry Smith and the crew of the *Today* show were already in town preparing to film the race. A front-page article came out in the *Napa Valley Register* with a picture of me, Will, and Matt.

As soon as we got settled, we headed off to Target to load up our Airbnb with snacks and water and other supplies. While we were there, a guy by the name of Judd Finkelstein approached us.

He tapped me on the shoulder.

"You're those guys. You're running the race tomorrow. You got hit by a truck!"

"That's me!" I said and introduced Matt and Will. We stood there chatting for a few minutes when Matt pointed to a button Judd had pinned to his chest that read: Be Kind.

"What's that all about?" Matt asked.

"Well," Judd began, "my wife, Holly, myself, and our daughters, Talulah and Ruby, were living in Manhattan a couple of years ago. One day our girls saw somebody wearing a button like this on the subway. They thought it was cool and said, 'We should have a Be Kind Day in Napa.' And so they spearheaded the effort and had a bunch of these buttons made up. Kindness is such a precious commodity. So what they do is wear them, and if somebody says, 'I like your button,' they take it off and give it to that person as a way to make a friendly connection. To make someone smile."

The more we talked with Judd, the more we liked him. Lo and behold, he just so happened to own a winery in town, Judd's Hill. So he invited Matt and Will and me—and our spouses—to go hang out as his personal guests. He spared no expense bringing out the wine for everyone, and I ended up buying a bunch of wine as gifts for friends and family. It was a fantastic experience leading up to the race. It felt so cool being recognized, being honored and respected for the journey the three of us were on. But more importantly, we now have a friend in Napa. We made a connection because we chose to embrace the moment, and so did Judd. He could have recognized us and simply walked away. But he didn't. For that, I am grateful.

Before we knew it, the day of the half marathon arrived. It started out in the fifties—a nice, crisp fall day. Perfect running weather. There were about 250 to 300 people who showed up to run. Definitely not the biggest race, but it had an intimate, hometown vibe to it. Beth and Jeanelle cheered us on from the sidelines. Matt's wife, Laura, ran with us, opting for the quarter marathon. The *Today* show had cameramen on bikes ready to film as we ran. They also had drones circling above to cover the race.

At the signal we all took off. I started out at a pretty decent clip. So did Matt. But Will was struggling to keep up with us. I was torn because I knew if I slowed down, it would end up dragging me down. And my goal was to get the race over as fast as I could, because the longer you're on the road, the more chances you have of getting hurt. Or wearing out.

But I knew he wasn't too far behind, so we just did our thing. Laura, Matt, and I ran the first 10K together. Before long, we got to the turnoff to where she was going to the finish line for the quarter. Then it was just me and Matt. It was getting hotter and hotter and hotter as the race wore on—low- to mid-80s. Our blue shirts were soaked with sweat and had white splashes of salt all over them.

To be honest, despite the *Today* show following us with drones and cameramen on bikes, and despite Beth and my friends and family cheering me on, and despite the fact that I was living out the goal that I had set within twenty-four hours of waking up from surgery, I was tired. Period. This was *really* hard for me.

There are only so many words in any human language. Certainly not enough to draw from to describe how much Matt's encouragement meant to me at that very moment. If he hadn't been right there with me, I'm not sure what would have happened. It was getting harder and harder to keep going.

"Go. You got this, Dean," he'd say, and somehow I found more in the tank.

Then he'd get about fifteen yards ahead of me, and that would push me to catch up. When we got to the top of the last hill, I could see the road ahead winding through a park. And around the corner was the finish line.

Seeing that finish line up ahead gave me the push to give the race all I had.

Whenever I run, I always give myself a number to hit. This time, my goal was to run the half marathon in under two hours. The thing is: I wear a watch, but I never look at it when I'm running. Seeing that finish line up ahead gave me the push to give the race all I had. I was determined to leave every doubt, every fear, every pain, every regret, every insecurity behind me. With about five hundred yards left, I thought *fuck it*, and I ran like I'd never run before. I let go of everything and sprinted with all I had left in my fifty-plus-year-old body.

I crossed the finish line and hit my watch: 1:59:55.

I beat my goal by five seconds. *Five. Seconds.* I was elated, but beyond spent. To this day, that was the hardest race I've ever run, including the New York Marathon. Matt was right there when I crossed. We hugged. We laughed. We congratulated each other. Then we realized Will wasn't there. We turned around and looked down the road. No Will.

My muscles were cramping up, so I grabbed some Gatorade. Just seconds earlier I had been sprinting. Now I could hardly walk. Matt took off and started jogging back down the road to find Will. I walked behind him, willing my legs to keep going. When I had gone about three-quarters of a mile, there was Matt and Will. We walked toward each other.

Will didn't look good. Not at all. "Thanks for coming back to get me," he said.

I smiled. "You stopped for me. Now it's our turn to bring you home."

Although none of us realized it, one year earlier we had started that journey together. And we were all determined to finish it together.

So me and Matt, we each grabbed an arm, and the three of us hobbled across the finish line.

The power of the human spirit lifted us above reasonable expectations, in that moment.

AFTERWORD

Looking back on it all, I wouldn't change a thing. Do you know why? Because the journey was so meaningful. The way my family rallied around me. The friends who I hadn't heard from in twenty years reaching out to me. The people I didn't even know sending me messages of encouragement and support. The devoted around the world praying for me and my family. The doctors, nurses, therapists, coaches, my employer … *everyone* was pulling for me, giving me their love and energy. It was like I got to go to my own funeral and see how people truly felt about me. That part of my journey inspired me more than words can even describe. And *that* is really what drove my recovery. It was like a flywheel—I was supported with love; I gave back effort. More love, more effort. Until the momentum had built up so much that I achieved my goal of running again.

> **Literally or figuratively, we're all hit by a truck at one point or another.**

The thing is: this story isn't really about me. It's about *you*. It's about your journey, your resilience, your ability to lean into the moment. Literally or figuratively, we're all hit by a truck at one point or another. The key is to find that hope and heart deep down to rise again. Sometimes that means leaning on your friends or family for their love and support. There's no shame in asking for help. We're meant to be connected with others. God knows we're stronger together than we ever are alone.

And let me be clear: rising from adversity does not mean being fortunate enough to walk again after getting hit by a truck. Sometimes injuries and trauma cause lasting damage, even with someone as gifted as Matt McGirt on call. Bicyclists get run over every day. Neurosurgeons operate on injured people every day who have little to no chance at ever walking again. Drivers accidentally hit bikers frequently. None of those events are unique. What was unique was how we were able to take each of our life's lessons—the positive ones and the painful ones—and come together. We did it together. Each man helped the other.

Rising means being able to move forward without bitterness. Without pride or hate or anger. There are plenty of folks I've met along my journey who weren't able to walk again because of their injuries. But they've risen just the same—in heart and in spirit. When I was laying there on Providence Road, Will standing over me, I started rising the moment I forgave him. I had no clue what the outcome was going to be. But I knew I wasn't going to let that accident destroy either of our lives.

Because I know I'm the passenger and not the driver, I gave everything over to God and defaulted to positivity immediately, in that moment. I set a goal not just to walk, but to run a half marathon and use the experience for good to help people. Matt made many life-defining decisions in the moment that enabled me to have a chance at recovery, then embraced the opportunity to connect with me personally, which gave me hope and motivated me. He was instantly a part of my life. Will sought me out immediately because that's who he is; he wanted to find me, apologize to me, and offer any help possible.

It's not about the destination—it's about the ride.

Life is a journey. It's not about the destination—it's about the ride. And let me tell you, my life has been a ride! My life was a ride before the accident. And the accident made me a better person. It enhanced my gratitude for humanity.

Matt says this whole experience has changed him as well. I obviously wasn't the first severe spinal cord injury he's had to operate on. And unfortunately I was not the last. But now, Matt engages and treats patients and their families a little differently than before our encounter. He's a man of science and obviously data-driven, though now he reserves just a little more hope for better outcomes, despite how low the odds may be. He sees no coincidence in the fact that the most uniquely optimistic person he had ever operated on also happened to have had the best outcome. Matt calls it the Dean Effect. I kind of like the sound of that.

So Matt now goes out of his way as a doctor to instill hope and optimism. He says that he will literally tell his patients, "It's going to be a tough recovery from this surgery. We're going to be positive, and we're in this together."

Will also says this experience has changed him forever. Sometimes, things just aren't black and white, good or bad. There was another motorist—a woman in her seventies—who had hit a bicyclist in Charlotte not long after my accident. Unfortunately, the bicyclist passed away from his injuries. Will happened to catch the story on the news. The woman's mugshot was splashed on the screen. She was being charged with vehicular manslaughter. *That so easily could have been me*, Will thought over and over again. As tragic as the situation was, the driver was not a villain. She was somebody's wife, mother, and grandmother.

Will was so deeply affected by her story that he wrote her a letter, basically telling her his thoughts and sharing his own story. She sent an email back: "I don't know how I would have made it through these last couple of days had you not sent me that letter. Thank you, Will."

He also says this experience has cured him of being such a worrier. The one thing he could have never planned for happened. That's why it's so important to always try to leave the past where it is. Let the future come as it may. And live each day, each moment, in the present.

The message to all of you who have read this book, and those who haven't: turn on your receiver! There is a power greater than all of us that is in control. If you look for them and accept them, the world is full of synchronicities—of wonderful, human, humane coincidences. Accept life on life's terms. And be grateful. Emmet Fox was an amazing metaphysical teacher, and his premise was that we are where our thoughts are. The only two things I can control in life are my attitude and my actions. When I am positive, positive things happen in my life. When I dwell on the negatives, things don't go my way, and I live in resentment. That is poison to my soul.

Get out there and help someone. It's the best feeling in the world!